*

*

Sonata in F# minor

*

Sonata in F# minor

Selected Poems

Barry Ivker

Cover art & inside illustrations by Barry Ivker

Grateful acknowledgements: some of the poems in this collection were previously published in the following publications: *Jewish Reel*, *Promised Land*, and *The Maple Leaf Rag IV*.

Published by Portals Press
4411 Fontainebleau Dr.
New Orleans, Louisiana 70125
www.portalspress.com

Sonata in F# minor
ISBN 978-0-916620-29-5

Table of Contents

Allegro

Andante Penseroso

Scherzo Doloroso

Capriccioso Guicosso

Coda

For Fran

Allegro Tempetuoso

Here and There

You said
The reason you did not visit
Auschwitz
Was
Out of sheer humility
In the face of those that died
In the face of those that lived
But
That was not quite true

You did not go there
Because you could not pray
There
Or because you were afraid
You might not be able to pray
There

While I
Who struggle
To find a way
To davvin*
Here
Make my pilgrimage
There
Night and day
In fear and trembling
And ask those that lie
There
To watch me dance
And humbly ask them
Whether my steps are worthy
Of their memory

*to pray

A Tale of Three Cities and More

The same women
Who would have earned their living
Fifty years ago
Watching children die
In Terezin
Smiled at this one baby
Tottering about this place
Today

It's good to chase a baby around this place
It's good to hear him laugh
Good even to see him trip and fall once in a while
And cry
And to pick him up
And turn his tears to smiles again

Good even to see the old woman smiling
At him
At me

People who come to marvel at the beauty of Prague
Sometimes come to marvel at this place as well
This hell
Nestled
In this peaceful town
There is a beauty here as well

Stars now mark
What might have been single graves
Had the bodies of the dead
Not been burned
And dumped
In the river over there

Stars and crosses
Separate
Arranged aesthetically

Centuries ago
They attacked the cathedral on the hill
Decapitating statues
Breaking stained glass windows
And then
Decapitated the decapitators

Old churches
New interiors
Silent screams on every twisting street

There is a story told
Of a monster
Created by a sage
Hidden away in an attic
In the old synagogue
Waiting for the call
To save the people from their pain

People come to this corner of the city
To see old buildings
To marvel at the tale
And they move on
Clay replicas in their sacks
For children to play with
To dream about perhaps

The golem did not make it to Terezin
He did not make it to the town in Slovakia
With the one survivor
Who shows visitors the house of learning
The sacred books still scattered on the ground
The gravestones used as paving blocks
The town folk professing ignorance
Of where their brethren disappeared
Even as they moved into the deserted homes
Even as they used the ladles to portion out their soup

We left that place on a train
Not a cattle car

Resting as best we could
Between the passport checks
The officers
With bureaucratic faces
And guns
That wake us
Through the night
The baby slept quite peacefully

Southeast to Budapest

People bustling about their business
As if there were no history
Beyond the martyrdom of Imre Nagy in '58

The baby marches in the open square
Midst giant statues of warriors and kings
Such vast spaces to explore
And he's not yet two
He flirts with everyone who will catch his eye
The locals and the ones on tour

They rolled a martyr right down that hill
In a barrel of nails
The pagans did
Right there
Where the boat sails
On the Moldau
In an hour or two

And there is the church
With the right hand of that saint
In the chapel on the left
That you can see for fifty cents
And you can kneel and pray
Light a quick candle
And then catch a quick concert
Where Liszt once held sway
Grab a pastry filled with goo

It grows cold and wet
Winter's on its way

We fly east over Auschwitz
To the center of the earth

En route to the Holy Land
Where they killed Moslems and more of us as well
They accused us of poisoning wells
Of desecrating hosts
Of using children's blood to bake unleavened bread
Of killing God himself

They cut us down
They herded us into our synagogues and
They torched them
They savored our screams
As if they were a form of nourishment
And then they traveled on
To slaughter Christians of another kind

Those of us they left alive
Fled
From England
From France
From Spain
From Portugal
Brazil
The smell of flesh burning
In autos de fe
Of mobs in ecstasy
My wife's own mother
Cowering in the cellar as a child
Every Easter Sunday
My aunt
Watching her parents
Cut down before her eyes
Stomped upon
Bludgeoned
Skewered

If I forget thee
Jerusalem
May my tongue cleave to the roof of my mouth
May my right hand lose its cunning
May my brain grow numb
May the image of the crucifix on the Charles Bridge
Dim
The Hebrew letters
Proclaiming the triumph of the Prince of Peace
Over us
And maybe them as well
The old women of Terezin
Smiling at this once babe
They would have watched
Burn to ashes
Fifty years ago
Floating down the river
By the Small Fortress
Where the prisoners were crammed
Seventy to a room
Or shot
Or transported to the East
More ashes
The old women smiling
At this one child
Safe now in Jerusalem
Safe
Long enough perhaps
To return here
Where the old women wait in their chairs
For another child to come

On Singing the Handel Messiah, Again

There is no other way
He said — you could sing all the notes in tune
Follow the dynamic markings precisely
And enunciate the words just so
And it would be pleasing
But not passionate

You must allow yourself to be moved
As if the piece meant everything to you
As if your life
Your very soul were at stake
As if you were suffocating
At the bottom of the sea
Plodding through an endless
Pitch black tunnel
And suddenly a brilliant light appeared
And you knew you were about to return to Eden
For all eternity
As if you were lost in a trackless desert
And an oasis emerged from the waves of unremitting heat
Beckoning with the promise of clear, cool running water
As if you were a true Christian
Or at least could act like one
For two hours or so
Well enough to affect belief
For those assembled
For the prelude to their holiday

I agreed we were all committed to turn notes to passion
To move the souls of those who came to hear it all

And then the images arose
Mainz 1096
They marched through our town with banners

Prelates welcoming
Einsatzgrüpen
As harbingers of The Second Coming

And there were Africans
Stuffed into the holds of ships enchained
While learned men debated
Whether profits were to be
Papal or Protestant
And what proportion of humanity it took
To be converted but not freed

And Amerindians marched
Onto barren earth to waste away and die
And internecine wars waged to determine
For all time
Whether bread and wine were fully or partly changed

These thoughts filled my mind
As I stood to sing the words

And a poet friend who watched me
From a front row seat
Noticed that I sang with fervor
And asked me how it felt
To be a Christian
At least for a while

I confess I did sing with fervor
And probably will do the same again
Next year

I can affect a sort of Christianity
And help move a crowd to celebrate
What they might term the spirit of the season
The message of the holiday

Shorn of course
Of all collective memory

And then come home
And celebrate myself
Silently
As Jew

Waiting

for Yoav Boaz ben Moshe Yisrael ve Rachel

Before there was a house here
Before the tree that bows to the wind
Put forth a single purple bloom
Before the men in the black hats and Kaffiyas
Gathered
To throw stones
Chanting mantras
In ancient tongues
I sat alone
On the Temple Mount
Waiting for a child to come
Waiting
In old Jerusalem

Before the chimneys and the cattle cars
The broken glass and the stiff salutes
I waited for a child to come
Crying for old Jerusalem

Before the Romans surrounded the walls
And the women, starving, beat their breasts
And the men blamed themselves with an old lament
I walked these stone-lined streets
Waiting for a child to come
Here on the hills of old Jerusalem

Before the altars where babies burned
And priestesses whored
And men cut runes into trembling flesh
And youths feasted on goat meat boiled in milk
And we hacked them to bits
By divine decree
I waited for a child to come
Here
In Old Jerusalem
By the banks of a stream
Fired by promises of transcendent love

Flint knife in hand
Standing by an aged wife
Laughing
Almost in disbelief
I waited for a child to come
Dreaming of Jerusalem

My hair turns grey
A small red clock marks the minutes
And the hours
The day is mild
Trucks and merchants join in barely heard choruses
Of vague cacophony
As I wait for a child to come
To replace the one that Eve lost
Once
Again

The tree bows before the wind
Purple petals fall
Stones are gathered
Mantras readied
For the Sabbath

For the child to come
To walk the streets of old Jerusalem

Apocalyptic

Jellyfish
Proliferate
More profusely
These days

Indeed
There may come a time
Ere long
When all that there will be to life is
One primordial, quivering
Mass
Filling up the universe
Ingesting the last roach
And fly
With no one left to wonder
Why
And how
All this occurred

To face the heavens
With accusatory mien
And say
This
Dear God
Is totally absurd
No one left to hear Medusans declare
We sting
Therefore
We are

Jenny

I do not recall reading anywhere
That Job played volleyball
With such passion
Or won a dance contest
Or cheered wildly
As his grandson
Rounded third for home
Or shouted
Kill the umpire
With lion's roar

Better Jacob then
Who felt
He was born too late
And struggled all his life to win
His rightful place
And
One dark night
Wrestled with an angel
Held on for dear life
Insisted on a blessing
And limped off at dawn
With a new name

All your life you wrestled
To the very end
And limped
Into the shadows
Finally
Jenny
Still
You laughed once when I told you
There was a table prepared for you
By the Man
Himself
Simple fare…
A plain white plate
A slab of bread

Italian
Freshly baked
And butter melted
There
On top
Just so
Just so

That's why it took so long
Jenny
That's why you had to wait
He knew
He'd better get the table set
Just so
Or
He'd never hear the end of it

And while you limped
Here and there
To watch your grandchildren
Come into their own
He got it right at last
You knew

You knew

One does not resist the call of such a love
When it comes
The fresh aroma
Of such bread

Jewish Reel

Well
Why not
If you are from Bucharest
And you find yourself
In Cork -
After all
If we learned to eat borscht in Russia
And gefullte fish in Germany
There are many ways to skin a cat
To style your hair
To grace a meal
To dress up
For the holidays -
You have to change a bit
Once you figure out
Where you are
This time
To prove to some of them at least
That you belong
To the others
Different or the same
Is all the same
So
We eat well
For a while
And dance
Somewhere between Bucharest
And Cork
And when the Brown Shirts came to call again
Shouting about Earth
And Blood
We'll start the process somewhere else
Again

Meanwhile
I must say
I've learned to do the Jewish reel

Like a native
So to speak
It's not so hard
I promise you

Somewhere between
The Vietnamese tango I once heard

And blue-eyed
Soul

Kiryat Shmoneh*

The children sleep in bunkers
Underground
They come out at break of day
To eat
To learn
To work
To play
They know the sound of rockets on the way-
Here and there
They watch for hawks high above their heads
Waiting to pick off one or two
As prey

In the center of town
Three tanks sit
Yellow, red and blue
Flowers wreathe their cannons
Children climb on top --
As if to say
Our worst dreams come to this
These beasts of some old war
Are quiet now
And tame
Here in the park they stay
We tell them what to do
And they obey

I wake at midnight
Now and then
Besieged by demons
Bleak and gray
Who wait to flay the skin from my
Flesh
Wait to display my broken spirit
To howling choruses
Barely held at bay

*A town in Northern Israel subjected frequently to Katusha rocket attacks from Lebanon.

26

I paint the demons
Yellow, red and blue
Round each bold neck I place
A floral lei
I give commands
And they obey
I ride them through my darkest hours
When morning comes
I let them slowly slink away

Mount St. Helen Stone

for my mother

It took minutes to destroy the peak's sym-
Metry, the ancient stand of fir and pine,
The old men who always seem to resign
Their fate to floods and quakes and waves — the whim
Of deep, dark forces of the earth and sky —
Buried under mounds of ash and molten stone —
The wisdom of bears and eagles, of flesh and bone,
Of falling leaves — and no one questioned why
The heat and force should turn sand hard and green
And crystal clear, with just a tinge of blue
Just here — something altogether new
For the newly pierced ears of one who's seen
Pain enough to be buried deep therein,
Yet greets each new year's growth with childlike grin

Nude Descending a Staircase

for Galia Nava

Gentle wave
Nude descending a staircase
She laughs
My mind wanders
From Eden
To Auschwitz

Mengele would have listened to her sing
Offered her a pudding
And put a bullet in her brain

An Arab woman walks on by
I measure with my eyes
And think of hidden bombs
I smile
I nod
I say Maah Salaam
Allah akhbur
She mutters in return
I wait for the gleam of a blade
I am ready to run
Back to this small garden
The rockets would never reach
This place

We walk on the promenade
Just above Silwan
Arab boys
Break branches from olive trees
People pass on by
As if this were a normal thing
Nothing to be upset about

The Golden Dome
Gleams
In the setting sun

We are in the open air
Exposed
We amble home

Galia is dressed now
In a gown
That glistens
She laughs
I smile
I play a game with her
Rules only a child of three
Could understand

And then
Suddenly
She is nude again
She sings quietly to herself
Like Eve did
In the Garden

She wants pudding for breakfast
An insistent, frail creature
Greeting a new day
I smile
I turn away

Mengele sneers at me from beyond the grave
I say Shalom

Auf wiedersehn, he mutters
In return

Ode to Sophia

I climb a mountain
To a cave
Where a guru sits
Like a lotus flower

Am I living well
I ask him —
In harmony
With the universe

A child will tell you
He answers
And he will say
No more

A child
I whisper to myself
And then I say
No more

On the eve of Mardi Gras
As I watch a parade go by
On Napoleon Avenue
In New Orleans
A friend appears
Two children in tow
The younger
Cute as you please
Catches the eye
Of the riders on the floats
Who throw
Beads
Trinkets
Toys
To her
She laughs
It is her due

Her older sister
Suffers from some nameless
Inborn anomaly
A timid child
Slow to learn
Wary
Midst all the hurly burly
And then suddenly
She accepts me as her friend
Her protector
The one whose praise
She listens to
As she catches this and that
And shares her joy
As her bag fills with glitter
Whom she lets garland her
With sparkle

She has chosen me
She has chosen me

I climb the mountain once again
I sit before the cave
My legs are stiff
I cannot hold
A Buddha pose
But I can sing an ode
Acknowledge the feel
Of one small hand in mine
The smile of a child
As she holds up
A strand of beads
And declares
To the whole world
I caught this
All by myself
I did
I caught this
All By Myself

Reflections on the Seventh Day of Passover

The Midrash describes
Twelve passageways
Through the Sea of Reeds
One for each tribe
Fish to be had for the taking
Gold and jewels
Washed up on shore

And for an encore
Pillars of smoke and fire
Leading
In a few short weeks
To Sinai
And
The Golden Calf

I think of my own Exodus
My wandering through the wilderness

Have I walked past
Bushes
Burning
Yet unconsumed
Symbols
Unperceived
Much less
Understood

A still, small voice
Drowned out by the roar of waves
Sweeping onto shore
Washing away lives like
Sand castles
Muffled by the scraping to tectonic plates
That collapse buildings
That bury children under kindergarten walls

I don't seek out miracles
Supernal darkness
Transcendent light
Waters turned from bitter to sweet

I think a single syllable
Would suffice
A whole sentence
Would be
Very
Nice

Jerusalem Day, 1990

The center of our celebration is
The very center of their chief complaint
Our dancing by the Wall without restraint
A painful twisting of the stream of history,
A wrenching pain, a frenzied shout.
A sullen, seething, stark display of rage.
A depth of hatred far too great to gauge
From those who very simply want us out
Of our Promised Land, our age-old fervid dream,
To tread these stones, to see these hills turn gold
As night draws nigh and ancient tales are told
And prayers are sung, and it would almost seem
That peace lurked in the shadows over there,
Not dark eyes filled with vehement despair.

The Shriek

for Edvard Munch

The shriek persists, even in the garden
Under trees heavy laden with ripe fruit.
The task complete, the lilt of lyre and lute
Leisures as dusk falls and the moon hardens into cold light;
And terror skulks through thorn-filled copses,
Waiting for her turn to play
Mother witch for children as they pray —
Their sense of safety nightly ripped and torn
Their dreams impaled on jewel-encrusted horn.
To live at best one's own best works refute,
The freshest growth lies withering at the root.
The final price for having to be born —
The saunter of a madman with a gun
Chanting old mantras in the noonday sun.

Celebration in Ḥevron

Babies are special
You don't count on them to pass
In front of your cross hairs
Every day
You don't expect them to touch the mail
You laced with anthrax dust
Just so
But when they do
That's very special

You want to horrify
To let them know
You're capable of atrocity
So they will listen
To what you have to say
Shudder
Back away

That's what we do
One baby
Two
Maybe down the line
A slew
Such grief around that tiny coffin
You don't get joy like this too often

Joseph's Tomb

Joseph made his people wander
To bring his bones from Egypt
To the Land

To Shechem
Where Dinah's rapist lived
Where her brothers took revenge
And slew every male —
A rough town even then

Last year
A hundred thousand Arabs
Give or take a few
Surrounded a couple dozen Jews
Huddled round the tomb
Guarded by soldiers ready to shoot to kill —
A situation deemed provocative
A powder keg ready to blow

So the soldiers withdrew
And that very day the crowds moved in
And dismantled the tomb
Stone by stone

And the world said
Nil

The next time you travel to the Holy Land
To see the sights described in the sacred texts
Don't look for Joseph's tomb —
It's not there —
Its stones line roads along the way
Much the way gravestones did in Europe
As soldiers goose-stepped their way through history
And people cheered and did their part
To wipe out memory

Joseph
Prince of Egypt
Who didn't want his bones to lie in foreign soil
Now lies under a mosque built in a day

Tough town Shechem
A tough place to live
A tough place to be buried in
In this Land called Promised
Once long ago
And perhaps in centuries to come
Again

Selective Poetry

There is a time for peace
There is a time for war
I do not know if this should be
A time of peace or war

I do know that somewhere
In Iraq a rocket is poised
Pointed toward Jerusalem
Toward my son
His wife
Their children
A baby in the womb

That if it strikes home
There will be dancing in the streets
Of Basra and Baghdad
Riyadh and Paree

I do know that there was no poetry
Written here to mourn
Kurds killed with poison gas
No poetry to mourn
Those that Assad killed in Syria
No elegies for the ten thousand Palestinians
Mowed down in three days in Black September
By their brethren in Moav
No dirges sung
For the six hundred blown to bits
Last year in Israel
For being merely who they were
There is selective silence here
A pall

And this I know
That if we had not gone to war
Back when I was just a babe
When that other one goose-stepped
Over the charred remains

Of those of us
He had within his grip
Dass die Dichter hier...
Wurden nun in Deutsch schreiben
Und ich wurde nur
Ein Windstoss sein
Vielleicht
Ein klein Gedenken
*Uberein**

*That poets here would be writing only in German and I would be a wind-blown speck,
perhaps only a passing thought

Marsaba—Saint Saba's Monastery—West Bank

I suppose I was being quite naïve
To imagine the hermits of that time
Constructing the monastery
Stone by stone
Into the cliff
In this forbidding wilderness
Alone
Eight hundred men
Dedicated to the glorification of God
Their way
Quite Byzantine
Which is to say
That as they contemplated
And as they prayed
The two thousand men they kidnapped
From the Caucases
To build this place for them
And thus did they
Have time enough and energy
To focus on theology

Six centuries later
The slaves were still on hand
When the Crusaders came on through
To rebuild from what was left from
Holy Wars with Saracens and Medes and Bedouin
And such
And that is what we see today
This monument to early Christianity

We are told to dress modestly
To show respect

The upper dome of the chapel
Gleams in the desert sun
Blue trim ensures the Evil Eye will hold no sway

A foreign architect today plans accommodating space
For pilgrims to celebrate
The one thousand five hundredth anniversary of this place

Soon
While down the road apiece
Descendants of the slaves
Green-eyed and red-haired
Calling themselves now slaves of Allah
Lead lives of a real austerity

Some tend sheep and goats
Some beg from the new tourists that pass
En route to marvel at the shrine

The awesome starkness of this place
Draws mystics from afar
To contemplate
To pray
And they will need the locals' skills again some day
Next time
Perhaps
They'll pay

No Pain So Sharp

For my son there is just Jerusalem
The place to live
To love
To pray
To savor an ancient tongue reborn
To breathe the air

For my sister every flower in due season
Is a vision
The black irises on the hill
The brilliant red of Caloniot

The place bespeaks poetry
It wells from the heart
It would expand to fill the world and all that live therein

My sister and my son
Alas

Golda said it best
There is pain in war
And loss
And death
But no pain so sharp
So unforgiveable —
To force such gentle souls
To fear, to hate

Two souls forever changed

I recognize the voices, not the tone
I watch their dreams now turn to stone

Just Down the Road Apiece

It's just down the road apiece
The sign tells you that
And somewhere there is a house
Where people celebrate the birth of a child
A man child
That my wife brought into their veil of tears

They would have us join them in their celebration
In a festive meal
They would assure us safe passage
They say
Through the shouting crowds
That call for our blood
That would celebrate to see us dead
All of us
Even those that bring their children
Into such a world, who
Will grow up to wish us dead
There in Ramallah
Just down the road apiece —
Where the soldiers fell today
And the crowds celebrated the deaths
With shouts of joy

Tadpoles and the Jewish Problem

My daughter spoke to me last week of
Tadpoles, of puddles surging with infant
Life deposited after the last
Rain by some dim-witted
Mother-toads.

Three days from now the puddles will be
Gone, she said, and only small black
Dots will testify to the passing fact of
Life.

And so we wavered with alternatives.
We had tried before to raise such creatures and we had
Failed after a week or so — but even a
Week of extra life was worth
The effort, said my daughter, and who was
I to disagree with such an affirmation?

But there was yet another way.
We scooped up hundreds in a
Jar and drove them to a nearby
Pond, where nature could take its
Course, where hungry fish and
Turtles and even insect larvae could
Eat their fill — and maybe leave a random
Two or three to reach the splendid state of being
Toad.
That night I lay in my bed, the history of our
People resting on my chest.
I thought of our small puddles of
Settlement throughout the ages, drying
Up under merciless
Suns.
How did we ever think to survive in such
Transient places?
How could we ever let our children come into
Being in the light of such imminent
Destruction?

How could we find ourselves in such
Spots that only random acts allowed for our
Transportation — to seemingly more
Pleasant places filled with waiting
Fishes, turtles, and even insect larvae —
All so that a remnant of our number could
Hop around for one brief season and
Reach the splendid state of being
Jew.

Jerusalem Stone

The hills glow at dusk
The houses are cut from the same stone

The Jewish houses

Arab houses are stuccoed over
Painted at times with aqua and salmon pink
To ward off the Evil Eye

There are villages of stuccoed houses
Where it is better not to go at night or day

The Evil Eye that once lurked in the dark corners
Now struts and shouts in the town square
In milling masses
Hurling fragments of stone
Large fragments of stone
At passers-by
Stone and concrete
And knives there are
Long knives and guns and sticks of dynamite — plastique

The stone holds the cold at night in winter
It is sometimes colder in than out
When the sun shines it is nice to get out

It is best to wear something warm
Something aqua with salmon pink

The hills glow at dusk
Anew
The Jewish homes as well

They are all cut from the same stone

Golda's Lament

When the rockets come
The children are led underground
The way they were in the Ukraine
When Easter came
Or when the S.S. came to call
The children saw it all
They grew like olive trees
Each twisted in his own way

In the basements there they huddled
Cringed
Here they wait for news of victories
Their minds racing through imagined fields
Shooting at invisible enemies
Trapped still

A half-shekel, please
A half-shekel a head
To atone
For having to be strong
For having to stay alive so
For raising children like olive trees
Twisted
Each in his own way

A Fence, A Wall

A fenced wends its way
Through the West Bank —
It separates fathers from sons
Predators from prey

Some say it's not a fence at all
Some say it is a wall

It is not the Wall I think of
When someone mentions the Holy Land

The Wall stands in Old Jerusalem
We face it when we pray
Stuff messages of hope in its cracks
Dodge rocks
At times
Hurled from the Temple Mount
By the other sons of Abraham

We dodge curses too
And spittle
And stones
And a chair or two
Directed our way by black-robed, black-hatted men
When they decide we are not dressed modestly
When we chant sacred words in mixed company
Or when a woman chants her songs of praise too audibly

Along Route 6 there is occasional sniper fire
From a rooftop or two
The fence looks like one back home
Built to keep the sound of cars and trucks from disturbing
The sleep of residents along the way
To let them sleep soundly and rise up fresh
To greet the day

Ululation

In Africa the women gather in circles
To mourn the dead and ululate
That's the way it's done

The men go off and slash banana trees
To vent their rage

At a wedding in Israel the other day
The groom's family ululated to express their joy —
Men and women both —
As the bride came in
And the Rabbi performed the rites
Then the bomb went off
And they buried all the parts they could

While down the road apiece
The family of the one who did the deed
Danced with his bits and pieces
Until dawn
Ululating ecstatically
And I went off searching
For a banana grove bigger than the sea
To cut and slash a bit
To set me free

And on the Road to Nazareth

for Gwendolyn Brooks

I understand how it was for poets then
Outrage sprouted
Like shabeens in Sophiatown
Like burning crosses in Birmingham

How could one dare to write about the spring
Or love or private loss or wrestling with God

Just rage
Just communal grief

It tests the muse to shape
Magna into sonnet form

How many ways to write an elegy
Di-versify the agony
So that each soul lying in the dust
Has its own face, its own history, its name

Another bus goes up in flames
On the road to Nazareth today
And seven more newly dead
Demand nothing less than poetry

And I comply — I must

And spring unnoticed slips on by
A friend celebrates a new-found love
A neighbor dies before her time —
Her children cry

I bury still-born sonnets with a sigh

When

Baruch drowned
Just about the time of
The Oslo Peace accords
Just about the time
The second Intifada
Was begun

They pulled him out
They gave him CPR

They shocked his heart
To start back up
Again

He breathes now
On his own
But
He is comatose
Unresponsive to
Words
Unresponsive to
Birds
And flowers
And the changing seasons
Unresponsive to music
To prayer
To his parents' voices —
Tight
Twisted
Trapped
In his own world

I see him once a year
When I visit
Israel
This year it seemed
His eyes followed
His mother's voice

As she moved
From one side of the bed
To the other
And back again
I am not sure
People ask me
When I think
Peace will come
To the Holy Land

I see images of bodies lying
Twisted
In the sand

Peace will come
I say
When Baruch
Sees his mother
Standing there
Beside the bed
And smiles at her
And nods his head
And says
Shalom

When the Time Comes

When the time came
I picked up my machete
And I went next door
To my friend's house
The one I walked with
Every day
To the well
The one who nursed my baby
When I got ill
The one whose baby I nursed
When her milk dried up —
She was one of them
I cut her down
Like a banana tree
And the baby cried
I cut him in two
And I went on
To those I did not know
So well

When the time came
I saw my husband sleeping there
Like a little child
He would always sleep like that
After we made love
I took the knife
The one I used
To cut meat in cubes
When I made stew
And I slit his throat
We were fighting then
And the war had only just begun

When the time came
I saw him standing there
By his wife and kids
The ones I played with
When I was young

The ones I fished with
All summer long
Whose mammy cooked for us
When company came
The one who worked for us
Who cut the cane
We strung him up
On yonder tree
He dangled there for all to see
What happens
To someone
Who's uppity

I guess it's something
You learn
Along the way
What to do
When the time comes

Nine Grains of Rice

I feel ill at ease
Three texts in Hebrew lie among the stuffed bodies
Of toads and armadillos and baby snapping turtles
And alligator heads and mammy dolls and porcelain masks
And whatever else will sell

Three volumes — a prayer book
He just used to pray
A book of laws and psalms —
The Ethics of the Fathers

This man — whose brother owns a Kosher restaurant
In the French Quarter
Whose son teaches in the Jewish day school
Whose cousin died
Blown to bits in the Holy Land —
Will print the names of my grandchildren
On separate grains of rice in Hebrew
And float them in baby oil
In small ornaments made in Israel
To adorn the throats of my daughter and my daughters-in-law
Will print the name of my nephew who lies comatose
In a hospital in Tel-Aviv
In Hebrew
Floating in baby oil
In a small ornament made in Israel
For my niece to wear around her neck
In a settlement in Gaza
That is shelled night and day
A settlement protected by soldiers
Under orders from the Prime Minister
Whom Europeans name the greatest threat to peace of all
Whom Hungarian poets accuse
Of turning the Holy Land into a killing field

This man exiled from Iran
Who left with not much more than the clothes upon his back
Who lost two cousins to bombers in the Holy Land

Who says there is no talking with people
Who bomb synagogues in Istanbul
While people pray
Who bomb the elderly at a Passover meal in Natanya
Who killed my cousin as she celebrated
Her anniversary in the Land
Who says Baruch Goldstein was right
He should have killed them all
In that mosque in Hevron
He should have killed them all

And I gasped quietly to myself
As he finished printing the names
On nine grains of rice in Hebrew
And floated them in baby oil
And sealed them in ornaments made in the Land
And gave me a discount of sorts
And wished me well
And wondered what I would eat at his brother's restaurant
In the Quarter in New Orleans
A Kosher meal of skewered meat

As people passed by and marveled
At the stuffed corpses of toad and turtles
And bought mammy dolls and never saw
The sacred books that lay there
Their titles face up for all to see

For me with my nine grains of rice
Safely home now in my drawer
Waiting
To adorn the throats of my daughter and daughters-in-law
And my niece in the settlement near Gaza
Full with child as the rockets fall about her
In the killing fields in the Holy Land

As the world snickers self-righteously
And waits for the Holocaust to begin again

What I Cannot Say

What I cannot say over the piles of corpses at Babi Yar
I will not say over the remains
Of a woman of ripe old age
Who dies in bed

The universe is not full or empty
According to the way the wind doth blow
Not full as babies first breathe the breath of spring
And empty as a soldier bangs their heads against a wall

The wonder is we breathe at all
And that we think and feel

I do not know if that's a call to poetry
Or prayer

But what I cannot say at Babi Yar
I will not have said
Over my remains
As I lie
Dead

O Blessed be the righteous judge
O Blessed be the universe

Prospects for Peace in Jerusalem

There is a mall in Jerusalem
Where they have taught Arab and Jew
How to shop together in peace

Fluorescent lights and neon signs
Expand tastes Pavlovian
Under the watchful eyes of guards with uzis

It is not quite yet Peoria
Not quite yet

Loudspeakers exhort milling passersby
To buy this thing or that
To buy many things
Many, many things

There is a secret plot afoot
A master plan

Peace will come packaged
In Styrofoam from Peoria
The trick is in the marketing
And when at last the last Shuk is closed
And there's a mall on every hill
With wide corridors and large parking lots
And big stores with big inventories
And fixed prices and credit cards
I will meet you there in Jerusalem
And it will feel just like home

Transformation

Sixty-five years ago
In the town square
In Kovno
The soul of a people was laid bare
They herded their Jews to this single spot
Clubbed and hacked them to death, sang and danced
They left them in the sun to rot
They yelled and cursed, cavorted, pranced —
I've seen the photos many times
I've felt my anger and my pain
Encysted them in plays and rhymes
Preserved my rancor whole, and then
Watched a woman from that place
Care for my mom with respect and love
I watched one hawk become a dove

Andante
Penseroso

Buddha and Me

Buddha sat at Auschwitz
On the roof of the shower house
Where he could hear
What he couldn't see
A rotund figure
In yellow robes
He rested in lotus position
His upturned palms
Upon his lap.
What he saw
He saw through half-closed lids
And he never lost
That quiet smile
That slight upturning
Of the very corners
Of his lips.
There is no difference here
He said from what I
Saw in India
Or China or Malaysia
Men dying
Together or alone
Preoccupied with self
Each frail existence
Screeching to a close
Sinking
In spite of all its protests
Into all embracing
Unity.
Unity of victims and executioners
Unity of the dogs
That sniff the edge of burial troughs
And the very earth they stand upon
Unity of Bo tree and oak
If man would stop a while
And think.

I sat with Buddha on the shower house
And heard the movement
Of bodies toward the door
Shaved bodies
Stripped bodies
The sound of scraping on the walls inside.
They did not look so different
When the living
Stacked their bodies up
For burning —
A few teeth more or less
A strip of skin missing on one or two.
Did not that mole
Under that left breast
Belong to a girl named
Tessie who used to
Write sentimental nature
Poetry and like
Her coffee strong?
The fire unified the
Bodies of the victims
And I paced the roof
While Buddha sat,
And muttered angry promises
While Buddha meditated.
I will remember Tessie's
Poetry I said
Bad though it was
And the mole beneath her breast
I will remember the hands
That placed her on the pyre
The name of the inventor
Of the burning process
And the post he holds now
In the new republic.

My eyes strained open
My mouth gaped in an
Ugly grimace
And the gasp that

Escaped me was not
Euphonious or
Buddha-calm.
I do not know where Buddha sits today
Or what he sees or hears
I think I am the only one
Who still remembers Tessie's poetry
The smell of her
As she joined the others
In essential unity.
My eyes still refuse
To close halfway.
My joints are now
Too stiff to form a lotus.

Just recently
I found another Tessie
In Bangladesh
Buddha's old stomping ground
If I remember history correctly.
And near the corpse I found
Some pebbles
Transparent
But slightly murky —
Buddha's tears they call
Them in this region.
This Tessie
After all
Was Indian.

Charred Memories

To build the new stand of houses
They cleared the place of trees
They knocked them down
They broke them
They left them in muddy piles
The bare trunks and twisted limbs
Like corpses
Stacked for burning

As people pass unnoticing
The smoke rises to swallow up the sun
The way it was
In Oswiecim

Charred memories pull at me in disguise
I look in vain for butterflies

These Mayans

Their house have changed little o'er the years
A bit of stucco more or less

Warriors used to come at times
And lead some off for priests to sacrifice

The priests are gone now

The Spanish came and killed some more
To save souls
They said

They linger on

Evangelists now come in droves
Their churches sprout like mushrooms here and there

While the old gods
Disguised as saints
Quietly accept old ways

And ages pass

They keep their culture
So
Their tongue
Their names

And wait for the next wave
The next pogrom
The next influx of strange, exotic views

These Mayans would perhaps make
Excellent Jews

Puerto Morales, 1993

Surely

I was uplifted by the recent news
From Eastern Europe and South Africa
Of people with little left to lose
Demanding freedoms that in America
Sprouted, we said, like native grass, like weeds.
Democracy, we smugly felt, was borne
From our verdant shores to fill the human needs
Of countless souls by tyrants' talons torn.
Surely the millennium was not too far —
We could reach it without another war —
Surely as old hatreds sown by ancient hands;
Surely as bombs set off by frenzied bands
Of terrorists and patriots counting prey;
Surely as cries of grief rising to greet the day.

Dilemma

for Harvey Bordewitz

Hitler listened to the Eroica with great joy
Perhaps he thought
The accolades
Beethoven removed from Napoleon
Were meant for him —
Perhaps he missed
The subtle hint the conductor had in mind
The hope that music
Of such a humanistic kind
Might change the Führer's
Murderous intent

Symphonies
I fear
Don't have that kind of power
Not a single Gypsy, Jew or gay
Owed his life
To such musical appeal

Alle Menschen würden Brüder
Perhaps
But those he gassed
Were untermenschlein in his eyes
So the poetry of Schiller
Simply did not apply

What is one to do
When an invitation comes to play
Beethoven
For those in Munich
Tsingtao
Lagos
Or Moscow

Music first
And then some beer
Or vodka

And if they liked the show
An invitation to return
And play some more
For those who kill —
If we don't return
Then surely
Someone
Will

And they might play
In such a way
That Beethoven's intent
Would be lost

Could a cadence
Convince
Anyone at all
That torturing dissidents
Is wrong
That genocide
Is just
Not nice
Unaesthetic
As it were

And if atrocities reach
A certain point
Where the effort seems
Futile
It is better not to play
At least not Beethoven
Not the Eroica

Why try
To get the Coda
Just so
The phrasing
The dynamics of a single note
As bodies prepare to fall
Naked

Into pits
Or ascend
In ashes
To the sky
Why even try

Better to be silent
To admit
That music
However inspired
Cannot stop an Anschluss
Cannot stop Einsatzgrüppen
From their appointed rounds
Can only amuse
Such folk
At best
As they rest
And prepare themselves
For the next day's work

Never — Here

We are shocked to learn that our boys
Forty-five years ago
Could have killed civilians by the score
To ensure that midst the dead
Was an enemy or two

We try to explain it all away
The confusion always found in war
The strain
The evidence is all too plain
They stood there
Guns in hand
And on command they blew them all away
Children
Like the ones they left at home
Old men
Kneeling there to pray

Our boys did that
Our men
And then they slept
And slept again
And waited forty years and more to tell
What their officers hid from view
The way they did in My Lai
They way they did in Wounded Knee

We are no worse it seems than anybody else
No one theorized
That slaughter with absolute calm
Was a sign of our superiority
That rising about guilt and shame
Would secure out name for all eternity
That visions of Übermenschlichkeit
Would somehow make our actions right

People with slanted eyes under foreign skies
They're not like us

We would never do such things
Again
Unless the circumstances were so dire
Who could blame a few for perpetuating
      an atrocity or two
It is not part of the character of our nation
That picnicked as black men swung from
      live oak boughs
As Injuns starved and immigrants cleared
      the swamps and died

Somewhere down the road apiece
Somewhere else
I swear
Never
Never
Never
Here

Images — Now and Then

The images I remember from Viet Nam
        most clearly
Are of one general executing a countryman
He deemed the enemy
On a public street in full view of a
        cameraman
Who dutifully recorded the act for all
        posterity
And of a girl of twelve
Her clothes burnt off by napalm
Screaming as she ran
Naked as the day that she was born
Hoping someone would end her agony

Such images embedded themselves
In the heart and mind

We knew the war took a human toll
On us, on them
And finally we called it quits
Leaving the ashes as they lay

This is a different war today
We use smart bombs now
Laser guided —
Cameras show pictures of smoke rising from building
Shown on diagrams and maps —
Commentators discuss technology
As if all this were just a game
As if there were no people there
As if bombs could select only members of the regime
The Evil Empire as it were
Since they were the defined targets
Not those who lived next door

And if perchance one or two got hurt or killed
All should be forgiven
For it was not intended

By next year the technology will be
            improved
The bombs will focus in on brain waves of
            particular men
And blast only them
And who would care if a photo showed their
            faces
Bleeding red
It would serve them right
And with such insight we could better sleep
            at night

The girl grew up —
A wife and mother now, they said

The man the general shot is still dead

Elegy for Father Karl Petersen

People will ask why
They will look up
To the Heavens
For a sign

You would have done so too
At midnight perhaps
When the world was still

And now you are
Still

They gather
Together
Multitudes
The people you touched
Holding on for dear life..
For dear life

Sign enough..
For true
For true

Sign enough..
It will have to do

The moon will rise tonight
At the accustomed hour
I hear the whisper of your smile
In owl flight

Us and Them

It was always Us and Them

Us worked hard for grades
And planned for college and careers
And assessed the attributes of appropriate life mates
And thought of safe neighborhoods to build homes
And planned for two or three children
Who would work hard for grades
And plan for college and careers
And would have fewer problems than we did
At that age

And Them were the nameless ones
That climbed the one tree behind our house
And fell and broke their arms
And climbed again
And turned hydrants on sultry days
And dropped out of school
And had children out of wedlock
And misused food stamps
And had drug problems
And danced with fervor and wriggled and thrust their hips
Like there was no tomorrow

We stopped going to the amusement park
Because it had become seedy
Grungy with Them
Arms draped around each other
Smoking
Throwing their quarters away in games of chance
To win stuffed toys no decent store would sell

I wandered through the City of Angels last month
From the tended gardens of the houses on the hills
To the pier on Saturday night
Where now they threw dollars away in games of chance
To win stuffed toys no decent store would sell
Their music was loud, alive

Black, Mexican, Vietnamese
A music of reckless abandon and despair
A music of passionate intensity

It costs three dollars now
To have your body whipped about and whirled
Two dollars to throw three balls at three bottles
To win something for a buxom babe or a screaming kid
While the music assaulted the ear
With demonic frenzy demanding a response

I returned to the guest house on the hill
To a wedding party where I danced with pure abandon
To music of my own and mused
That there ought to be a music for Us and Them
To celebrate our lives, our kids
And the pain that creeps into the best tended gardens
Somewhere between the gardens and the pier
Between propriety and the rigged games of chance
With their stuffed animals and clowns
Turned out in some sweatshop in some Third World place
By workers with vacant stares
Too tired at the end of the day
To wriggle much of anything at all

The Logic of Terrorism

Because someone in the government
Passed a mosque with ill-disguised disdain
Because a policy enacted late last year
Agrees with that of one of our declared
      enemies
Because the vernal equinox draws nigh
Because three times three times three days
      have passed
Since the last infidel met his end
Because because has seven letters in English
And two less in Spanish and one more in
      French
Because the rain falls mainly in the plain
And B and P are voiced and voiceless
      consonants
Of a labial variety
Because no one checks baggage on trains
The way they do on planes
Plain planes
Not plain trains
No one complains
And the moon waxes
And the moon wanes

Our green thought in this green season
Was to plant ten bombs in Madrid
One morning during rush hour
On a train
So that the whole world would come to
      understand
The justice of our cause
Two hundred dead because leopards have
      claws in their paws
I pause
The iron laws of divine justice permits no
      flaws
No hems, no haws

We saw the mayhem that we caused
And found it good
As you should
But instead
Bled red everywhere
Arms here and legs and hands there

Today Madrid
Tomorrow watch where your feet may tread
For if we find a pretext you're next
And whatever the season
When you see the flash you'll know
We had a reason
We always have a reason
We always do

Just People

In Yemen the ornate knives the Arabs wore so proudly
Were made by Jewish silversmiths
Who by Moslem law could wear no knives at all

In Israel the knit kippot the pious wear
Are made by Arabs the zealots wish would disappear

Red-necks live in towns
Named for Injun chiefs their fathers slew
They hum the music of the men they hanged

Artifacts of cultures spread throughout the land
It's just the people we could never stand

Birmingham, Alabama — July, 2000

I bought a sno-cone
Yesterday
In front of the church
Where
Forty years ago
People met and
Changed the world
It's all chronicled
In the museum
Across the way
I was tempted therefore to say
There is progress here
No doubt

Then I thought back

While these streets seethed
With hate
Despair
That summer
I was —
Elsewhere

In Sarajevo
Where folks
Twenty years before
Slaughtered each other
On sight —
The city in which a million died
Was peaceful at long last
And I was tempted to say
This was new
And there was
No turning back

And then it all began
Again

The rape
The torture
The fear
The killing was almost
Cavalier

I sipped my sno-cone with a straw
Mango and passion fruit
Combined
No one seemed to mind

I was tempted to say something
On this street
Where things were now
So mellow
So friendly-like
No matter who you'd meet
Except for fags and queers
Some locals said —
We'll hang them high
While children picnic on the grass
And watch them
Die

Lamed Zayin

The mystics looked out upon the world
And found it filled with such pain
They felt
By all rights
It should implode
Once and for all
That very day
But that very day
The sun rose in the east
As if nothing special had occurred
And this was difficult to assess
In a world created by Divine decree
In a world maintained by
Justice
Mercy
Grace
Even if God chose
To hide his face
There ought to be some clues to discover
Some message
To unravel

And finally they explained it
Thus

Thirty-six righteous men there were
Willing
Or assigned
To bear the agony
Of each and every
Calamity
And thus allow
The seasons flow
The birds to sing
New life to appear
And grow
And if even one among the thirty-six would die
And not be replaced

Instantly
Then
The universe would end
With a single word
Or perhaps
A sigh

And having answered this perplexity
The mystics heaved a sigh
And penned a pious poem or two
Dedicated to
The One on High

I suppose
The answer that they gave
Was just as good as
Any other
But for the fact that
All the thirty-six were
Men

Thirty-six
Twice eighteen
Twice Ḥai
Twice life
The square of three
Multiplied by
The square of two
The number seemed
Complete

Yet
It seemed
There could have been
One female soul
One woman
Who knew what it meant
To suffer
For all humanity
One woman

At the very least
Walking through some carnage
In some bleak corner of history
Of her story
That would be included
In that crew

Men can suffer deeply
But women
Bleed
Men shed their seed
But women
Fruit
And then they bleed again

The number thirty-seven is prime
We'll have to work the logic out
While there's still time

Dyed in the Wood

I - Better Red...Iroquois

They are so pale to have discovered
The color of poppies and columbine
Of hummingbird throats and woodpecker crests
And leaves of sumac in the fall

So pale to have devised colors such as these

We traded them furs for their dyes
To help us express in full measure
Our joy of living in this place
We captured it in the blankets and rugs we wove
On the leather we covered with bold designs

They have the land now
They hang our blankets on their walls

We search for colors now
To paint the full measure of our emptiness

II - Better Red...Navajo

They told us our designs were too subdued
Too somber to be popular back East
Where the big money was
And then they left us to our own devices

We used to unravel English blankets
To get the red
The red the British got from Spain
The red the Spanish got from Mexico
Just over the ridge of those mountains there
From Indians like us

And then the new dyes came
Bright and permanent
And our weavers went wild

And they told us
No
We had to tone things down a bit
Pastels were now the rage
Wan
Like the moon rising over Salem and New York

Our rugs are selling now
Pale echoes of the blood of spring birthing
Of the summer hunts of years gone by
Faint memories
Of leaves about to fall
Before the snow comes blustering in
And drifts of whiteness cover all

III - If I Forget Thee, O…

The first time they led us from our shores
To another kingdom
They had lapis there
A different kind of blue
We could not dye the corners of our prayer shawls then
And every time we'd chant a psalm
The flavor of exile passed over our tongues like gall

To some it tasted sweet enough
The lapis…blue enough
Bluer than the sky at noon, they said
Bluer than pain
Bluer even than memory

After a time they bid us all return
To rebuild all that we had lost
And some did

The Temple
I've heard it said
Was even more glorious than the one before
Gold, silver, bronze
Cedar straight from Lebanon
Purple, scarlet
And a different blue

Some things get lost
No matter what you do
Which small shell it was
And how to make it yield its color to the thread
Some things get lost
A thousand years or two
And then perhaps
Are found again

There is a mosque upon the temple mount
Filled with tiles colored a different kind of blue

I wrap my prayer shawl about my head
And dream about the way things were
The way that they could be

At the corners now
A thread of blue

I stand here in Jerusalem
Rocking slightly to and fro
There is nowhere else to go

Dance Suite

I - Like a Hungarian

It took a while to learn to play the violin
Like a Hungarian
He said
Now that the Jews and Gypsies are no more
      Once we gathered them all up
      And they were shot
      Or gassed
Someone had to do it…
Weddings
Christenings…
Who else was there to mirror
Our collective soul?

I studied what recordings I found
I learned as best I could
And I am pretty good
For a Hungarian

The Gypsies and the Jews are gone
Our old ones slowly die…
Who is left to tell?

I teach my brother's son
He plays with fire
His eyes so closely set
You'd think he was Romani
Or perhaps a Jew…

Weddings
Christenings

He will play for me when I am gone
A rhapsody to set my soul dancing on its way
Up there — like a Hungarian

Up there
Or down

The sound of countless violins
The tunes I first heard when I was three
Played with fire by a Gypsy or perhaps a Jew

II - Spanish to the Core

That is the mountain, he said
The very center of the world...
I went there as a boy to learn to play
From the masters that were left
After the flames burned heretic and Jew and Gypsies...
Those that distilled the Moorish beat
Haunting and cryptic and...
Spanish to the core

Stand on this hill
Enjoy the view
While I play for you
While I dance for you
Echo
The very heartbeat of the world
As we hear it...
The very heartbeat of the world

I played for my grandmother just before she died
She smiled at me...
You have Gypsy eyes, she said, and Marrano blood
And somewhere a Berber horseman gallops
        through your soul

I stand tall and proud upon this hill
Guitar in hand
My heels strike fire upon the stone
My steps echo the very heartbeat of the world
Spanish to the core

III - America's Music

It is America's music, he said…
He meant Jazz and Blues
Not Indian…
Standing by that tree
Where a piece of rope still swung
Lightly in the breeze
By the river with a long, Indian name
In a town with a long, Indian name
With a high school whose symbol was a chief
Or a tribe that was no more

He played a mean trombone
And made the rounds of local clubs
And could high-five it like a brother
When he had a mind

It is America's music, he said
Standing by that tree

I still hear the screams of the Black man
As he sizzled that Sunday afternoon
And the folks gathered round
For fried chicken and iced tea
And leaned back in the growing shadows
To hear that mean trombone intone
A bit of America's music

Stairs

The stairs of the temple are steep and tall
Imposing, treacherous
Climb them at your own risk
The sign says
Beware

I have spent my life at the foot of stairs like these

I watch an old man ascending
A fat woman in shorts who waddles as she climbs
My children scamper up
My wife methodical

Any style will do
Athletic
Tentative
Reverential
Straight up
Winding like a snake —
A rattlesnake
Ah yes
One at each corner
In stone
They watch you as you climb

They have seen it all
Jaunty strangers
Victims
Stupored
Led by learned men
Seeking answers to arcane mysteries
Revealed in patterns of the stairs
Or in the rain that falls —
Patterns in a serpent's coils —
The unpatterned life is hardly life at all
Every movement, every gesture
In harmony with the heavenly spheres or
You climb at your own risk

And the snake strikes
Home
And terror reigns
And rains
And reins

The stairs are steep and treacherous
(My children romp
My wife climbs steadily)
I wait heart in hand
Moving timorously

Step by step toward the stone altar
A voice in me chiding
Not like that, you fool
Not in fear and trembling
Bound up these steps in a single breath
Take in the view
Dance with joy in the face of death
David danced
Isaac walked a steady pace
Three days
Climbed onto the altar himself
And lay there as the knife hovered over him like a snake
To cut him to the core
Dance
Dance before the lord of this place
Ascend

The going up proves easy
Descent is terrible
Looking down at where you've been
To where you must return

I go down backwards
Step by step
By the chain
Holding on securely

The snake
So the legend goes
Descends headfirst
Then quickly rises once again
Heavenward

My dancing is earthbound
By earth bound and tied

They tied the hands of prisoners
Captured in raids
Stripped
Marched to the steam houses
Starved for two days
Drugged
They ascended
Step by step
Never to come down again
The priests laid them on the altar
Face up
Staring at the sun
Broke their backs
Cut their still bleeding hearts out with an obsidian blade
Drank their blood
Feasted on their liver and their lungs
Dozens in their turn

We have our photos taken
By the jaguar with the playful smile
(They laid the hearts there on his back)

We smile for posterity
To say that we were here
We and the others climbing various ways
Smiling at the top
(The serpents smile as well)

I did not smile at Gamla
Where the Romans without ceremony pitched infants out
Onto the rocks below

At Babi Yar
At Buchenwald
Remember when you went forth from Egypt
Remember Amalek
Remember
Chichen-Itza
Remember the shower houses
The steam houses
Feel the pain
Remember the intricacies
The efficient modes of death
Remember

We climb
The sun is high
The sun in whose name all this was done

They raised young girls to anticipate with joy
Drowning in deep pools for the glory of God
Trained men to compete for the right to lose their heads
For the glory of God

We are here walking up the steps of the temple
So elegantly, so precisely built
We are here deciphering the dreary tales of death

Small dark men and women
Stripped naked
Spines snapped
Disheartened

If I forget thee O Jerusalem
If I forget

The view is wondrous from the top
The descent is awesome
I used the chain step by step
Backwards

Always backwards

Not like the serpents smiling at the corners of the temples
As we mortals come and go
Waiting for the ceremonies to begin again
Here

But any place will do
With or without windows to catch the fleeting sun
The moon
The stars

God help us
Guidebooks in hand
Cameras ready for a smile

For posterity

Any place will do

Chichen-Itza, 1993

Jan Hus

Jan Hus stands tall
In the town square in Prague
Surrounded by the churches
Of those who did him in
Five hundred eighty-five years ago

He wanted to bring the Bible back to the common man
You didn't do that then
You might as well have been a Jew in 1942

No monument for them
Yet
It might take a century or two
Or four
Maybe 2442
One more gaunt figure will stare across this square
And catch Jan Hus' eye
And even then few will tell you
Why there were Jews back then
And empty buildings now

You can visit the Jewish Quarter
Of course
It's on the tour
They will tell you
That
In the attic of the Altneu Shul
A man of clay sleeps
And waits to walk these streets again

Start with Jan Hus
He'll say
And work your way through history
Red drop by red drop
Stream by stream

There is truth etched upon his forehead
And sometimes death

You stood in silence
He will say
You watched them get on the trucks
You watched them get on the trains
You watched them starve
You watched them die
You smelled their flesh as it burned
Centuries of ash falling from the air

If Jesus lived in Prague in 1413
He would have been burned at the stake
If Jesus lived in Prague in 1943
He would have had typhus
He would have been crammed with seventy others
       of like mind
In a tiny cell in the small fortress in Terezin

He would have been shipped to Auschwitz
Gassed in one of the shower houses
His body incinerated
His ashes would have settled out into
The winter mud
And on the third day
There would be nothing left of him at all

The Kamikazi in the Rock Garden

I am drawn to these people
There is a vision here
A harmony

I could leave my hectic pace in a moment
Spend hours in a rock garden
Put down the myriad bits of color
I coax into complex patterns and gaze contentedly
At white glazed vases filled with flowers and blades of grass

I stand in awe of a few brush strokes
That define a space, a time

I am drawn to these people
Who hunt whales to the point of extinction
And decimate other people's rain forests
Who will let no one call this place home
Not descended, as they are, from gods
Who turn Zen into Kamikazi
Who shrug their shoulders and turn away
In mild embarrassment
As stories of their rape and pillage greet the day

I walk through rock gardens
Hold white vases to the light
Silent centuries cupped in my hands
As a Kamikazi bows politely
And a geisha pours out my tea

I dreamed once of making a pilgrimage
To the country where Tagore once wrote
To study the philosophy
Here where hordes of men pushed other, darker men south
And raped their women and labeled their offspring
Untouchable
And called the process karma
Here where millions live in squalor
And people pass them by philosophically —

For they say they'll have another chance
Another day
To move on up
Or down

And I wonder as I breathe deeply
And rid my mind of all imagery
And feel the tension flow out from my fingertips
Silent centuries in my hands
As an old Albanian nun closes the eyes
Of yet another desiccated child
Beneath the quiet smile that plays across the Buddha's lips

I walk the streets of old Jerusalem
The city of peace
That we face collectively
As we pray each day
We who stumbled on a new belief
Some millennia ago
That all life was sacred
Unique
Who wrestled with a God
Who loved us like a mate
Who made contacts with us
With all peoples of the earth
Who fostered choices
Who followed each step of our destiny sternly
Compassionately
With ultimate concern
And bade us to share this vision with the world

Along with holy wars

Our students labeled us reprobates
And spread their holy wars around the earth
To our very doors

I chant the melodies that haunt my dreams
I gloss texts that challenge my soul
I brush past men in black garb who call me ignorant

Irreverent
Because I do not bow and groan the way they do

I wonder silently as I dance
About this brusque intolerance

And I write
Filled at times with great delight

A child in me claps his hands with purple glee
While another in the shade
Is filled with sickly greenish dread
He tenses, tightens, lashes out
He bites his thumb
He faces doubt
Awkward, stumbling and inept
Every failure nursed and kept intact

Every joy met with disbelief
Every bond tottering at the edge of grief

I dance on
There is a fire that stokes my soul
I touch others and they dance as well
Centuries of wisdom in hands and feet

I dance slowly in a rock garden
On the road somewhere between Jerusalem and Mt. Fuji

A kamikaze waits for me

He bows politely as we sip our tea

Mississippi Man

I am a Mississippi man, he said
I cross streets when I come to them
Whether a car is speeding toward me
Or the coast is clear —
Cars have brakes
They have drivers
That don't want dented bumpers
Or blood on their windshields
Or higher insurance rates
Or guilt-ridden memories—
They will find a way to stop
Or swerve, or skid, or not —
You can only die once
And there is a limit to pain —
I know that
I am a Mississippi man
I was conceived through rape
I was born with the cord wrapped tightly around my neck
Some said that was a warning
Of things that could come to pass
If I didn't watch my step
But
I was too busy to watch my step
Too busy leaping and cavorting and climbing trees
Too busy jumping buck naked into fast-flowing streams
Too busy letting the flavor of yams and watermelon
Drip down my chin
Too busy noticing the shape of women
Of every color and shade
To be careful —
I am a Mississippi man

I love the sound of singing
And poetry
And blues
More than the sound of teachers droning on
Telling me what to do and when
I love the music of mockingbirds

And the soaring of eagles and buzzards
And the silence of cats on the prowl
And the sight of children doing cartwheels
One right after the other
I love the wobbling steps of babies
And the grace of gymnasts
I could slice through a crowd of tacklers on a football field
For the sheer joy of running and feeling my own hips
Swiveling and my body juking and the earth beneath my feet
I could dance and I could love for an hour or a week
For a year or two
Forever
I am a Mississippi man
Don't tell me what is permissible and what is not
Don't tell me who is off limits and who is not
Don't threaten me —
My grandfather dangled from a tree
For having eyes that wandered
That's what they told me
From the time that I was small
They made me jump through hoops
And step and shuffle and kow tow and scrape and bow

They beat me in the schoolyard
They beat me in the bushes
I watched myself bleed and I watched myself heal
And grow strong like a gnarled oak

I sent my roots deep and my branches spread
And opened to the sun with so much green
You couldn't paint it all on one canvas
I am a Mississippi man —

I see where I am going
I head for it straight
I walk through cow dung in my path
Up your front steps
Across your white carpets
And right out the back door

I don't step aside
And if there's a street I have to cross to get anywhere
I'm going to cross it
And any car that's headed my way
Better stop or slow down or move around
Or get his windshield splattered
It don't matter to me one way or the other
We all get splattered somewhere down the line
Like my mamma when I was young —
But I keep charging straight ahead
Singing some fool song or other
Steady
And strong
I am a Mississippi man
A Mississippi man

The Child and I

Philosophy begins
At the edge
Of the collective pit
They say

I went there
Night and day

A child lay
Face down in the mud
For all to see

Make sense of that
I say
Some do

I am tired of making sense

Someone wrote once
That that was the beginning of
True wisdom

I feel no wiser now then a child
Lying
Face down
In the mud
Well before her time

I carry her with me as I go
She comforts me
When the western wind blows needles
Through my brain

Tell me about the wind
I pray
About the rain
Tell me

About
Death
And pain

She tells me nothing much at all
She is a comfort
Still

I asked her once
What she might have been
Had they spared here from the mud

A philosopher of sorts
She said
But she is dead

I pluck the maggots from her head
My throat is sore
My stiffened socks lie idly
By the door

II

Tell me about Heaven
I asked her once
In pain

Heaven is like dancing for a while
She said
Leaping
Landing softly
In the snow
Remembering
Fondly
How the music
Was

It sounds a lot like here, I said
When things go well

Heaven is what people dream of

When they make of life a hell
She said
And when they can't let go

A fly buzzed twice about my head
And are there flies up there
I asked
Swinging at it wildly with my cane

Flies clear the air
And then the dance begins again

We danced a while
There
In the snow
The girl and I
And one persistent fly

III

I walked about
One afternoon
Through heaps of slag
Through slums
I walked along the open graves..
My feet were sore

What can I do, I sighed
There is work enough for a million men
Until the end of days

Write a song she said
Find a purple flower
For me to see

I walked on and on
Till I came to a mountain
I could walk no more

Climb she said
I will tell you where

I climbed high
Into the air
And halfway there
I found a clump of flowers
Purple as the dawn
And a bird
With a worm
Sang to me
Mournfully

Pick one flower, she said
To put into my hair

I carried her down
The song as well
I sing it to her sometimes as I dig

The purple flowers are now spread
Among the graves
For those like her to see

I sing to them
They sing to me

They sing of purple things
Of grieving birds
And worms
Of death
And poetry

Until the very end of days
Purple
Death
And Poetry

(9Av, 5758)

Then and Now

In the beginning was God
And She was black or red or tan
Before somehow He became white

That said, the search is on
To discover the pristine
Old world purity in people
Especially of the female variety

As if Astarte
In her procreative frenzy
Did not demand the mutilation of her men…
Or parbroiled babes

As if the Ashanti
Did not enslave tribes they overcame

Or Apache
Midst acts of reverence for the earth and her creatures
Did not maim the bravest of other clans
With weapons of primitive grace

It will take more than the dyeing of the skin
To make me whole again
More than a gender shift to reach gentility

We are all murderers and have been
Since the first

Murderers and progenitors
Who stop to marvel at the color of the dawn
Enroute to slashing babies from the womb

We dance for the demise of foes
For pure joy
Carve arabesque on clubs
And teething rings

The first footfall of man
Brought art and death
And trees plowed under
Black, red or tan
Or white

Then
And Now

No noble savages we
Or noble lords

Or ladies
Fair or swarthy

Earth mothers
Or the children of the dream

Just
Us
Then
And now
Searching
Half-heartedly
For Tao.

His Wife Died

He sits always in the same chair
Near the back door
Staring into space

His wife is dead
She died in this place
In this nursing home
He was supposed to leave weeks ago
But they treat him kindly here
And he has nowhere else to go

His wife died
He says again
He may talk about the weather
If another resident comes by
Or about the food
He may — when the sun is high
Go out to watch the ducks in the courtyard
He may smile a smile or two
And then return
To the same chair
By the back door

His wife died
In this place
His wife died
And this is home now
They treat him well

He stares into space
By the back door
On that chair

His wife died
Don't you see
His wife died
And she is
Dead

For Gus and Chris

I'd like to ski
That slope again
To flex my knees
To feel the hill

I'd like to read that poem
Again
To let the words caress my tongue
Like fine liqueur

I'd like to touch your thigh again
To feel the throb and flow of moments shared..
The darkness
And the glow

I am betrayed
It seems
By life itself
Gone crazy at the core

O let me hear your voice again
Til I can hear no more

Waltz of the Flowers

I've lived in shadows since the dawn
The lilac scrim of mourning light
The child lies crying out of sight
Afraid her heart will turn to stone

The love I offered now is gone
The graves marked off in black and white
And as pain blossoms in the night
Death greets me with a tired yawn

But there were moments in the sun —
I waltzed among the flowers there
My mother wove them through my hair
I thought the battle then was won

I pray to God now he will bless
Me with a long and peaceful sleep
Too often he has seen me weep
Too often seen me in distress

In me He made the perfect fool
A curio to pass on by
They mock me as I moan and sigh
It takes too long to learn to die

Amusement Park

People wait in lines
In the sun and shade
For the momentary thrill of
Remembering tomorrow how it was —
Strapped in
Hurtled down
And spun
Hours spent
For minutes lived
Until someone pulls out the plug
And the lights die
And there is nowhere left to go
But home

Scherzo Doloroso

The First Six Million

The Rabbis say that six million of us more or less
Died in a single night before the Exodus
By Divine decree
Those too weak to risk the parting of the sea
Those for whom leaving was a low priority…
And having noted this small footnote from our history
The sages discuss at length
Those who coped with freedom to some small degree

The shelves are filled with volumes on the Holocaust
But not a single one on those first millions lost
Scraps of meat from the Divine molars flossed
At no apparent theologic cost
To those by the more modern trauma tossed

As if only the acts that demagogues commit
Are considered fit for outrage
For earthquakes, fires and plagues with which we're hit
The message from our texts is to submit
We'll know at last the reason for our woe
Why these six million had to go
In the dead of that one night
We'll understand it all
Eventually
Or maybe not
Maybe we'll choose not to know
To preserve the pain

There are times when it seems there is meaning
Enough in darkness
When the price of passage seems too great
Perhaps I left my Egypt just a little bit too late
Burying too many lost souls that one night
The taste of manna doesn't seem quite right

Or

That's what they say
Each child stillborn from the womb
Desiccated, raped and burned
Grieved in some ethereal domain
Each sparrow's fall
Each locust in the swarm
Each mating pair of love bugs
On a trucker's grill
Will evoke an elegy
Or
Nothing much at all
Tadpoles in a fleeting pond
Plankton gobbled by the score
No less
No more
Than people on a flooded plain
Mourning in the failing light
Ready to give birth again

And still she prays

Don't complicate the issue with theology
The words are there, codified by centuries
Of sages who faced their own adversities

It cannot be that there is no meaning
Beyond private pain

She prays three times a day
Facing East toward Jerusalem

She prays to a God that hears prayers
That searches the human heart
That cares for every sparrow ripped and torn

She prays fervently
Looking toward a Temple that is no more
As if a single missing word would collapse the universe

And return us all to primal chaos
As it was in the beginning when God said
Let there be light
And there was light
And He saw that it was good

Another Day

Before the ashes stopped smoldering
The transformation was begun
From Temple to Yeshiva
From Priest to Rav
From ritual to ritual
From rite to rite
And life went on
Catalogued
Enumerated to the second —
When words could still be said
Pinpointed
To a drop of blood in a chicken's egg
To a golden hair on a reddish mole
All power and honor given
To the interpreters —
Healthy children
Rain in due season
Milk and honey
Prophecy
(No — That smolders still)
Truth lies in heavy tomes
In the fine print
Intoned by bearded men in long black coats
Doubt filled up olive-sized
Placed carefully in dusty drawers
For Elijah in the end of days

The Temple has been rebuilt
To the last golden hook and loop
It still holds sway

While off somewhere
Far away in a field
Some strange fool in motley dress
Spouts poetry
Dances wildly in the open air
And thinks it prayer

And God laughs
And laughs
And lets the sun come up
Another day

Tisha B'av, 5753

Alignment

for Ellie, May he rest in peace

If I am diagnosed with some terminal disease
I will not spend my last days eating
Rice cakes and almond butter
Balancing yin and yang
Being temperate and wise

I will eat all the dark chocolate I can get
Let my endorphins float me toward the grave
Let the malignant cells proliferate as they will
Let my organs fail one by one
I will be too busy dancing with Matisse to notice
Surfeiting on Bach fugues
Letting poetry roll over my tongue
Drip down my chin
And fall
Drop by drop
At my feet

And if anyone suggests that my aura needs a realignment
While I'm second-lining my way toward death
I will direct him to some nether region
Of some imaginary space
Where he can contemplate his navel for all eternity
Subsisting on rice cakes and almond butter
Without a hint of chocolate to flavor his blissful
Nothingness

Everyone Pays

The story goes that Moses made it to the mountain top
With a bit of prodding now and then
Aaron went part way
The elders just a bit
While the rest waited on the plains below
Warned to keep their place and keep it well

And no one did

Some aimed too high
And some too low
And everybody paid

There is no voice today
They say
To designate exactly where on the mountain
Each of us may play
When to wrestle
When to ride the winds on chariots of gold
And when to walk humbly
Like Bunsche
Waiting, naked and craven
For the blue crystals to fall
Again
While voices whisper
Weeping
In the glowing darkness

Everybody pays

Everybody pays

Eclipse

The ancients would have been awed at such a sight
The eye of heaven slowly winking shut
A heavy portent this
A Divine response — at the very least —
To something of significance
Some act called for as the eye opens once again
Some deep acknowledgement

But our own sages tell us in advance
Exactly when, how long, the color and the shape
How much is known, how much to be discovered
Offer us the choice of witnessing their accuracy or not
Much like a guide granting us the option
To pass by a building somewhat off the beaten track
And, after slowing down a bit, continuing on our way

We chose to slow down a bit in the clear night air
To witness the accuracy of our sage prognosticators
The bites of insects who joined us in the watching
The heaviness of our own lids
Which weighed down upon the following day
Somewhat more lasting than the residue of awe
Even as the days go by

Our sages promise us another such sighting
Before the year is out
Whate'er we do

A non-response to nothing of particular significance
No act called for
No acknowledgement

I'll give an upward glance
If I happen to be out

Foretastes

Somehow I missed it
The raft poised at the top of the chute
I thought was the foretaste of something
      really wild
Around the next bend in the tunnel
Through the mountain in the darkness

I looked ahead
I prepared myself
Only to find that the tunnel
Was the peaceful afterlude

The chute was it

And I
Who charged down the white water
Churning
Seething in fury —
I looked forward to nothing much at all

We rode the river once
Never to return again
You can never raft the same river twice
It is never the same river
It is never the same you

We were guided through sites
That bespoke the glories of things past
Whole cities —
Each stone contained a tale
We just might want to know

We walked on through at a measured pace
Promising ourselves we would return
And listen to the stones more completely
      next time

But that is not to be

We will go elsewhere
And walk on through
And make other promises
We will not keep

Quick tours of Effysus
Quick tours of Cappodocia
Of Pamukkale
Of Istanbul
Of marriage and parenting
Quick tours of life
Foretastes of a meal that we will never eat
In our journey through incompleteness
In our rehearsal for a play that we will never stage
Going round the bend for the final thrill
Only to find that we missed it in passage
And it was really wild

It All Depends

On display on the far wall
Of a shop on Ben Yehuda Street
In Jerusalem —
Two nuts charred, half-melted

They barely missed us
When the bomb went off
The owner said
Thank God
We're still alive
      Not like the others
      Maimed and dead
      Just outside the store
Thank God

Gratitude begets theology
For those who manage to survive

For the others
Theology begets grief

It all depends on
Which way the metal flies

365.25, More or Less

Corn grows more or less as the rain falls
In due season, or won't
At times we eat our fill
At times we don't
The land bakes hard under the eye of heaven
The soil crumbles into dust
Or just washes quietly away
Seedlings rot or wither
As we count our steps
Take the measure of our lives
As stars wander
And shadows lengthen on the wall

Three hundred sixty-five and a quarter
Is a number to be reckoned with
Hard to figure
Hardly divisible
We formulate
We fall short again
We begin again

We will get it right this time
We will
We must
Or we will have naught to blame
But ourselves

If we place the objects on the bed in such
and such a way
Like the stars on such and such a night
In syzygy
We could rest easy then
When the moon got full
When demons dance with hideous grins

God
It is so hard to get the numbers right
(Bite your thumb

Draw blood)
We deserve admonishment
Rebuke
It comes like morning dew
Or not
By whim
By fate
By reason of the gods
By grace
Every move
Attuned to the harmony of the spheres
Or not quite

We calculate again
As the corn lifts its head to the sun
Or won't

Count the steps to the altar
Count the words
Calculate the arc of the priest's arm
Adumbrate
Daub the blood just so
Effectuate
The rain
The demons lurking in the shadows
Kept at bay
Just so
Or we are lost
Again
The gods will hide their faces in a minute
They will not be mindful of us
Our faults
Our fate

The soil crumbles
The corn withers
Or rots

We have not reckoned well
Three hundred sixty-five and a fourth

Indeed
We have not reckoned well at all

Remove the dead
We will get it right this time
We will cut and slash again
Precisely this time
Or the demons or the gods
Or chance
Chance

Hush your mouth, I say
If you cannot count
At least your heart, I trust, is in the right
        place
We will daub your blood
Just so
Sow the corn
So the rain
In due season
In dew season

Lord of the Universe
It is so hard to get the numbers straight

Not a Prayer

Commandments imply a commander
That's the rub
Affirming that God is One
On the shores of Sri Lanka after a tsunami
A God who intervenes in history
In children's lives
Who loves sparrows
And listens to people pray
And cares about anencephaly
And wants us at least to keep
Separate dishes for milk and meat
And will allow us to use
Antelope horns for shofars
To usher in another year

And if this not be so
Why not enjoy a lobster tail or two
Something that I will not do

My sister prays at the bedside of her son
Comatose for half a decade now
She puts tfillin on his head
While he lies there twisted
All but dead
It is the thing to do
To is written so
Pleasing
To the One on High —
She stares into the Heavens above
Or looks inwardly at a place I cannot sense

I look up
I see the sky
At sunset or dawn
The sight is worthy of awe
And poetry
Not prayer, at least not for me

I focus on a leaf of grass
Pushing up through sand and mud
New life stubbornly green
Producing seeds that scatter in the wind
Now that the tsunami is but a memory

Puzzles

for S.R.

There is a logic to the process
And a solution
A feeling of completion
Once all the boxes are filled in

A satisfaction
To know
That one's intelligence
Was more than adequate
To the task
To the next puzzle
Most probably
As well

Beckoning
Like some illicit drug
Like some cultured whore

While in the next room
Chaos sits plumply on the floor
And leaves an excremental stain
You try bravely
To ignore

When the Eye Itches, Can the Mind be Calm

(an African proverb)

And was it
Providential
He mused
That the fibrinogen coalesced
Exactly at the point where
Gray stuff begets
Theology
A cruel stroke
He now termed
Fate

And thought about a universe where
Pigs had wings
Where altered sulphur bonds
By chance
Lead men to worship
Happenstance

Where God bustled just outside consciousness
Without a prayer
Listening to trees fall
In virgin forests
Alone
Prepared at last
To crush the world between
Metaphoric fingertips
Inconsolably intoning
Phrases of the Song of Songs
On transcendental lips

Yitzhak's Proof

He is eighteen
And he wants to justify God's ways to man

A God who the tradition states is involved
With his creation, with his chosen nation
Every moment
Sustaining galaxies and molecules
Or not
Caring, guiding, intervening
Or not
Directing and yet somehow still preserving
        man's free will

And everything that happens
For apparent good and ill is a function of His will
From a splinter to a Holocaust
A fallen sparrow
A generation lost
As he says this his eyes glow with fervor
And mine with fear that he will somehow
        prove to me
That suffering and pain have some purpose
And were that so, I know that
In a minute I would storm out of my Shul
Like some damned fool
And tempest tossed
Something in me would be forever lost

I do not do philosophy
I want no proofs of anything at all
No hints of cosmic meaning or significance

I will settle for awe

That we are here at all
That Yitzhak has the wherewithal
To be so logical

135

That we are prone in spite of all
To learn
To celebrate

I celebrate Yitzhak for his acumen
For the glow and fervor in his eyes
For his faith that he can prove
Beyond a shadow of a doubt
That Providence can co-exist with choice

I celebrate myself as well
My outrage
My eternal grief
I celebrate my disbelief

Scylla and Charybdis

The choice she has is to be in pain
Or stupor
There is not much room to sail free

The doctors come
They click their tongues
They shake their heads
One has to die some way
And she is nearly ninety-three

The pain shatters memory
The drugs induce sleep
She can barely take a step
She can barely raise her head

The doctors say she has lived long enough
This is no time
To contemplate heroic acts
To pull her through again

I say even a ship of death can sail calmly
Toward the setting sun
Can give the helmsman one last chance
To watch the sky crimson and then turn grey
One last chance
To feel one's feet
Balance the waves
To celebrate passage
And know that it was good

Wrestling with Zen in Warsaw, 1941

As the Germans came with cannon
And with flame
And scan our bodies
With calm disdain
I muse
I meditate
I take a gun
And aim it
At least at one
And acknowledge
As I fire
That I kill myself as well
Even as I consign his soul to Hell

Even as the building falls about my frame
And I acclaim
The Lord our God
O Israel
Is
Lying by my side
A bullet in his brain
With no one left alive
Who even knows
His name

After Nantahala and the Everglades

You cannot see the reflection of the moon
On the waters of the Nantahala
At midnight
Any more
They turn the river off at dusk
They turn it on again
At dawn
To let the people raft the waves
To master the
White water —
Wild water
Surging over random rock formations
Below

One day
Perhaps
They'll model the flow on a computer screen
And mold the rocks as well

It's still possible to get a thrill
Riding down a simulated stream
Still possible to get a sense of what the Everglades was like
Once
Before they fixed the level of the swamp at a foot of water
Above the muck and mire
Still possible to get an idea of what passion was like
Before they trained us to enjoy
Virtual
Love.

The Beach at Natanya

A nice beach it was
Even in winter
With the cold and rain

Nicer than England in January
Someone said
Or Holland
Or
Germany

Nicer than Russia, too.
And so
Immigrants come here
Many do.

And the town grows apace

We walked the paths
Up on the cliffs
And then we walked
Down to the beach
And looked for things
To tell us we were
Here

The shells were
Unexceptional
There was seaweed
A dead fish or two
A dead sea turtle (small)
Some cans
Some condoms
Some nicely contoured stones

Some concrete blocks
To keep the waves
From eating at the cliffs

Some signs of history

Of the refugees
Fifty years ago
Smuggled in
To the promised shore

This was not
Then
Just
Another beach

And as we walked
And thought
A bulldozer raced on by
And disappeared
Round the bend

And we walked on
And it returned
And passed us once again
A dead Hereford
In its iron jaw

Our friends ask us
On our return
How it was to tour the Land
Now
With all the troubles there

I tell them with a shrug
It was just fine
That they should come
To wander there

But if they wish to bathe or get a tan
At Natanya's beach
They must watch
For falling cows

Bemerkungen

I.
Les bosches viennent jusqu'ici
Les biches
Fuient
Achtung, Petain
Envoi-moi vos juifs
Aujourd'hui
Toute de suite
Les galaxies
Attendent
Dead meat.

II.
Orbits are predictable
The sun will explode in
Five billion years
Over Sudetenland
Not tomorrah
Schade

III.
Thirty-two times
Verdi
In Terezin
En route to the East —
Over the cattle cars
Les petites étoiles
Twinkle
The many eyes of
God

IV.
Babi Yar
100,000 more or less —
Fewer
To be grammatically strict
Rules can't be changed just to accommodate
Atrocity

V.
Les corps putrisce
Les vers fleurrissent
Le bon Dieu est
Endormis
Tant pis

VI.
Cranes migrate over the
Life boats
Subject for an elegy
Gory
It's true
But a source of inspiration
A poet's glory
On reflection
Somewhat whorey

VII.
Buchenwald
Trees and books explode
Jüdenrein
Überein
Liebfraumilch
A vintage year
Yours and mine
Really, really
Fine

VIII.
Grey, black, white
Guernica in flames
Picasso paints the walls of
Oswiecem
Cyanotic
Red and green
Rainbow promise
This was not a flood
Just a lot of gas
And blood

IX.
The war was o'er
When I was four
When I was nine
My home team lost the
World Series
And I cried
For dreams that died
Flies laid their eggs
On the remains

X.
Ants feed on limp watches
Heldenlieder in Dachau
Bayreuth
Darfur
It all makes sense
Göttendämmerungen
Gods die
Periodically,
Les hommes restent
All zu menschlich

Elizabeth Fleischmann

She died in 1905
Almost unnoticed
An obituary in the local news
An article on her work
Five years before
And that is all

She was the first to use X-rays
To help surgeons find shrapnel in soldiers
Wounded in battle
The first
And at the time
Apparently
By far the best

Of Roentgen I could write at length
But not Elizabeth
She had her brief moment in the sun
By the time she got the cancer from her work
She must have glowed

I don't know the color of her eyes
Her hair
Whether she was filled with hope
Despair

A woman
Mere Fleisch and bone
Worthy of a verse
Her life
Purposeful and terse
More blessing than curse

And so an elegy
An ode

I heard that she was
Pigeon-toed

Fat Tuesday

Plastic madness
Drives bankers and chauffeurs
To feign nobility
To throw seeming stuff
To the crowds below
Piles of stuff
Amassed
Assessed
And just as well
Forgot
The greed is real enough
The shouts
The envy of those
Recognized
From above
And lavished on...
What did you get?
Something longer
Shinier
More ornate
Worth a push and shove
A bared breast or
Dick

Plastic reigns
Till midnight
When the streets are cleared
Cleansed of
Stuff
Of bags
And beads
And drunks
And bells ring out
To announce the start
Of plastic
Lent

Fat Wednesday

The beast that stalks
Tender flesh at night
Out there
Where the sidewalks end
That rips and tears at
Innocence
Out beyond the sacred grove
Walks upright once a year
At noon
High spiked
In drag
A flaming faggot queen
Prepared for frenzy
Ultimately
Unamused
By the

        blasé bacchanalcans he spies
        who tear their goats apart
        on cue
        quite
        comme it faut
        giggling as the flesh
        twitches
        wiping splattered blood from brows
        demurely
        bumping
        grinding
        quite securely
        ogling just enough —
        having fun

Fun, he shrieks
Fun
It was not like this before
I have seen grandes dames in rut
Shamelessly ripping at the clothes of men
I have heard them moan
I have seen widows and orphans
Raped in courthouses

Lewd dances in church corridors
Clerics cavorting with maidens and
Corpses
Hitting at each other with
Murderous intent
I have seen it all —
But fun
Fun sticks in my craw
It chokes my very soul
So proper they
As the pipes of Pan do play
      in peasant garb
      picnicking on well-groomed lawns
      cleansed of
      pigeon shit
      de-loused
      de-fleshed
      feigning excess
      so responsibly
      so obediently
      that
      at the witching hour
      all merriment doth cease
      all evidence swept off the streets —
      by morning
      naught remains to tell the tale
To shout
That I exist
Out beyond the sacred grove
Where the sidewalks end
Forget me if you will
I'll teach your errant sons to
Kill
On clean swept streets
In the pale moonlight

Freak

Three score years and ten
A freak —

A specialist figured him out one day
And fixed him up
Sort of
Sexually —
Ambiguous no longer
A male now
Pure and simple
Free to act
According to his destiny
Forty-five years a clerk
All but unseen
He came out with a bang
One day
Fondled three breasts
Patted four butts
Exposed himself
And ogled like a fiend

And was fired
Arrested, castigated
Jeered at, spat upon
Incarcerated
And buggered in turn by three in-mates

And through it all
Till the day they broke the bottle o'er his head
And cut his throat
And he bled onto the shower room floor
Four-foot five
Hump-backed
His stubby fingers caressing the tiles
One last time
O mother mine
Through it all
He smiled

Gut Response

Dean Swift was disturbed
With the workings of his beloved's gut
But not the workings of her vagina

Was sex for him
Somehow more spiritual than excretion
Did he wish her nubile
But rectally dysfunctional

Lawrence
Two hundred years later
Bought the whole package
Kidneys
Colon
Cunt

Mellors did not mince words
Thar she spits
And thar she pisses
Like a natural woman
He loved his Connie for all that
He fucked her proper
And she felt raised on high

It says in Scriptures
That on the sixth day
God created male and female
And it was good

A paean to vaginal secretions
And the flow of menstrual blood
An ode to the workings of the gut
An ode to every orifice
May it function well

And pity poor Gulliver
Swiftly
In his private hell

Homage to Rabelais

Calling someone an anal aperture
Ought to be a compliment

Knowing when to open
And when to stay shut

Infants don't yet have the skill
We have to clean the mess they make
The sick, the old have lost the knack
To their chagrin

When someone shoots his mouth off
Or keeps it shut
When he should speak out for
Himself
Or someone else
And we suggest
That he is a sphincter
Lying
Between the nether cheeks
We should amend the epithet
And say
He is a defective valve
Diarrhetic or
Constipated
Not knowing when to keep his waste in
And when to let it out
When that skill is learned and
Mastered
There is a sense of fundament —
At well being
Of harmony and peace

So
When I am saluted with such an epithet
With no objectival additions or
Accoutrements
I'll take it as a compliment

My sphincters still work well enough
Thank you
Both hither and yon
And I'm glad you recognize
My accomplishments.

Homage

The top of Nat Turner's skull
Lies somewhere in Chicago
His skin binds a
Family bible
In his home town
An heirloom
Brought in for
Show and tell
In a Kindergarten class

Pieces of the noose
Cherished
Like splinters of the cross

The bones — of those that hanged him
Now molder in the grave
But Nat's remains are
Preserved
As if he were some nameless Jew in
Essen
Part of some bride's wedding ring
Some hausfrau's wig
A lampshade
In an attic space
To be discovered
In a distant age
And sold for thousands
At an auction

It's Nice to Have My Bladder Back Again

The person that I call myself
Pees in a certain way
This is not perhaps a subject
For an epic
Or a tragedy
But be that as it may
I lost my sense of self the other day

I lay there on my back
My legs like lead
I could not move my toes at all
And they cut me
Effected a repair
And then they let me be
To recover
My integrity

It took an hour to feel my feet again
To flex my knees
Another hour before I stood and walked
Such joy

But the bladder was
Another matter
I could not sense that it was mine
Until day nine
No matter how sublime my thoughts might be
Reflecting on my mortality
This alien presence
Joined me in the stall to tell me
I was not quite there at all

And then at last I was again

On Sunday
In the afternoon
I danced all night
Beneath a crescent moon

Lost Marbles

When I was ten
I once shot marbles at a nickel
Propped against the curb
On Brighton Sixth Street.
The local kids
Cheated me out of my nickel
And my marbles
Too

It's no fun to lose one's marbles
At any age

My Uncle Bill
My friend Ray
Don't know where they are
They don't know the time of day
When the last visitor came
Who their wives and children are —
Not a marble left
Between the two of them

My mother tells me
She is falling apart
She can barely walk
She tires quickly
She needs help to dress and bathe
Her hearing is dulled
And she can barely see

But she has all her marbles
She can reflect on everything
She ever said or did
And panic
At the very thought of death

I have collected marbles all my life
I lost a few after the hurricane
But they are replaceable

My knees are shakier
My teeth are cracking
My body is subject to strange new
Symptoms
Ailments
Without a name

I think back to those marbles I lost
When I was ten
If I had been wiser then
Perhaps I'd be a bit wiser now
Closer to something like
Philosophy

My Unlawn

A lawn
By definition
Should be uniformly green
One species of grass
Alone

My neighbor has a lawn
My plot of earth
Won't
Qualify

An olio of grasses
Weeds

Like the grounds around my house
When I was young
I'd mow the place
And leave a secret square of
Tiny flowers

One day I counted
Fifty-three kinds of insects there
On my small plot
And I felt
Justified

Today
I celebrate
Randomness

Honeysuckle vines
Grow over bushes
Smother then with fragrance
Virginia creepers
Line the walls
Carpenter bees
Nest in the eaves
Woodpeckers bore holes in the sideboards

A family of raccoons
Call my attic
Home

I am unkempt
Uncouth
I sing of tiny purple blooms
That in spots
Crowd out the grass

And
At the very edge
Of my neighbor's lawn
I dance

Mardi Gras, 2012

The drama
Such as it is
Is
On the other side of town
The crowds massing
To see the floats pass by
To catch trinkets
Tossed
Or thrown

A friend of ours got bonked on the head
With an ornamental
Commemorative
Shoe
Two teenagers got shot

While we
Munched peacefully
On
Sushi
Sipped miso soup
Green tea
Then listened to some
Folksy songs
Sung to a select few
And retired for the night
To screw

What will you do
Mardi Gras weekend
A teller asks me
We'll think of something
I say

Shabbat morning
I will chant
The Torah position
And we will eat

A Kiddush meal
And if the weather holds
We will go to a parade
Endymion

We will play the game
Like Christian pagans
As we have done
For years
Two score

And on Fat Tuesday
We'll stroll
On Bourbon Street
And Royal
Marvel at the costumes
Of transvestites
And realtors
And before the clock strikes twelve
And the faithful ash their heads
We will be back
In central Alabam'
That's where we stay
Since Katrina came on through

We nibble at frenzy
Neatly
And well before the madness ends
We slip away
Discretely

Martin and Hannah*

You would think that people of such intellect
Probing the essence of being and knowing in the universe
Would know enough to
Recognize
The essence of
Horniness

All that Platonic obfuscation about
Initiating students into the world of speculative
Philosophy
Came down initially
To a stiff prick
And a receptive orifice

Couched afterward on a bed of German
Polysyllables

As if wisdom and
Mutual regard
Flowed from arousal and release —

Well
Didn't Plato say
That eros marked the difference between
True dialogue and
Mere rhetoric

A willing student
With comely breasts and thighs
Responding to an ardent teacher
Always ready
To make a point

*Martin Heidigger and Hannah Arendt

Nor'Easter

Only six died
The Mayor said
The storm could have been much worse
But God was kind
He wrote that to the mothers of the dead
It is not recorded
What they said

Ordinances

for e. e. cummings

It is the season for the Bradford pears to
Bloom
Thickly white
Luxurious
All over Birmingham
The Magic City
The City of Trees —

Except on the median strip on
Highway 31
Where they once blossomed a bit too
Expansively
And so
Some official
Dutifully
Had them all cut down
In the dark of night

It is enough to make the Werthers of the world
Contemplate
Suicide

All those officials
Ordinances and power saws in hand
Busily creating
Emptiness

But
They cannot stop the Spring
Theycannotstop
The Spring
Theycannotstopthespring

And that must drive them mad
Goad them on
Until they find another ordinance
To lead them to another spot

Sacred to memory
To produce
More emptiness
To show their children
Proudly
And say
I did that

Their children
Who
At an early age
Practice writing
Ordinances
So that
One day
They
Can
Change the orbit of the moon
So that
One day
They can block out
The very sun

Perspective

A bad year for shells
She told me —
No hurricanes

Some years ago
After Denis
In this very spot
The crop had been superb
Tulip shells and baby conch
Murex and cones
She used for her designs
For making
Angels

Angels
Formed from molluscs
Churned up by the waves
Cast up on the shore
To die before their time

Cherubs —
Pretty little things
Like poems
Inspired by tragedy

Slim pickings
She said again
No tulip shells for the angels' wings
I'll have to make do with
Augers
And whelks
And wait for the next blow to come

I thought it might be nice
To give an angel
To some friends
To guard what they salvaged
After the storm came through

Ah
Katrina
She said
Now that was a good time for shells

Very good

In fact

Superb

Question

Six miles to the North of us
Fifteen miles to the South
Tornados cut a swath
And where we were
Near calm
A short, slight rain

Friends call us from afar
Thank God, you're safe
They said
Were we just North or South
Would they have said
Thank God
You're dead

Scallions

I forgot to buy scallions she said

I don't eat scallions I said
They give me heartburn and acid indigestion

They add flavor to the slaw
She said
It's a new recipe
Six ingredients
And I forgot this one

I'm sure the slaw will be
Just fine I said

And she replied
I don't know what could have been going
Through my head
I knew I was to make the slaw
I knew all the ingredients
And I forgot the scallions
I did

No one will miss them I said
Your mother is no fan of green onions
Either
Especially if they're raw

I can't believe it
She said again
No green onions for the slaw

Tell me about your work
I said
She did
And it was going well
And she was poised
Confident
Professional

Tell me about the children I said
And she did
And they were doing well
Poised
Confident
Intelligent
Filled with the joy of being
Just themselves

And then we talked of other things
The community, politics
The world at large
The universe

And then she said
Again
The scallions
I forgot the scallions
Six ingredients
And I forgot the one
That makes the flavor
Full round complete

She is wont to remind me
Of mistakes I made in parenting
Twenty-five years ago
The scallions I left out of this or that slaw
Along the way
My daughter
Romping with her kids
Healing furry creatures
Chanting sacred texts
Fighting for the rights of man
Dressed smartly in bright colors
Celebrating womanhood
Poised, confident

And only one bunch of scallions
From total happiness

So Visceral

You read about things like that
Sometimes
Studies about
The impact of music on
The milk production in
Belgian cows
Or salamander fertility
Or roses
Or ferns

Now this
The impact of the classics on
Bile flow
On pancreatic function
The sound of strings
They say
Stimulates
Liver enzymes and
Gastric juices
The way Nature
And Nature's God intended
While heavy rock and rap
At least in this regard
Cannot be defended

I listen to a symphony now with new regard
I listen well
I never knew that Mozart could be
So visceral

Visions

She sees ducks on the ceiling
Generic ducks
And maybe
Fish

Is this a sign
An intimation
Or ju
st a symptom
Pathognomic to her
Infirmity
Just a quirk of
Physiology

The ducks come and go
Swimming here and there
Without rhyme or reason

Ducks
Not
God

She is sinking slowly
Into her private pond
For an eternity

The ducks by then will
Fly away
To swim on another ceiling
Down the hall

Ducks
Not swans
Or pelicans

Ducks
Not
God

Searching for Tao in Vail, Colorado

Tao
Someone called it
Recognizing the power of water
The surge
The flow
Riding it to shore

Recognizing the pull of the earth
And taking the hill
Just so
Just as it presents itself
Moment by moment
The earth yielding its secrets
The body
The spirit as well
To anyone willing to venture
To the very edge
To hover
Between ecstasy and stillness
Between raw panic
And sheer delight

I approached one of these philosophers
I, one of the more timid folk
Whose moderation was born of inhibition
Whose joys were circumspect
Still circumscribed by memories
Of childhood fear

Teach me
I asked him
How to venture to the edge
Teach me how to hover
Between ecstasy and stillness
Between raw panic
And sheer delight
Teach me
Tao

A puzzled look came upon his face
He shrugged
Later, man
And chugged his brew
There is this lady, see
And I'm about to score
Again

He looked at me
And he would say no more
He was preoccupied, it seems
With searching out the Tao of sex and beer

I'd have to wait for him
Another year

Walt Had it Right

It seems so obvious —
An enzyme misaligned
A synapse stilled
And the qualities we define as soul are gone

A man mistook his wife for a hat
Imagine that
Unless you've had a stroke
And no longer imagine much of anything at all

Consciousness fled
Perhaps to Heaven or outer space

The eye sees
That's what it does
The ear hears
The brain thinks
And I am awed
I must admit
Awed beyond belief

That's why I dance
And I will dance until my knees give out
Or I forget the steps
Or the impulse to my limbs is mute

If I know what's going on
I'll sigh
If not
Look for me soon in the ground beneath your feet
The grass —
Walt had it right
A green finale to all earth's delight

Capriccioso Guicosso

Aftermath

for Herman Berlinski

I wanted to hate
Her
For being so clearly
German
So me-
Ti-
Culous
So loving of her native tongue
Which, as it happened,
Was yours as well

I watched you chatting —
Landsmänner
And felt jealousy
Wanted to lay claim on you in a
Language we both learned from
Other than a mother's lips
A language of shared pain they
Mouthed at your direction

Did you shout at the Germans you shot at
In your native tongue
With rancor
Or imperious calm
Or perhaps with lyric sadness
For the years of separation from your beloved
Leipzig
Where Bach played
And windows gaped
And men went forth
To blitz Poland
To herd people into cattle cars
To march through France
Where you survived with gun in hand
And shot to kill —

Leipzig

Which opened the doors of Johann's church
      to you
And honored you for the music
Which sang of those that died
From Leipzig
Layered and limed in the pits of the Vaterland
Am Visrael
Ḥai

Kol Yisrael
Ḥevrah

All' Leipzig eine Brüderschaft
All' Deutschland
All' die Menschen
Und die Kinder
Auch
Sechs millionen
Auch

Zehn tausend vernichtetenwelten
Auch
Menschheitsgefühl
Weggeworfen
Menschheitsmateriell
Verbaucht

Ich muss etwas warten
Bis ich mein Ekel überwindenkann
Vielleicht ich kann dein Machingewehr
Eine kurze Zeit borgen
So dass ich auch in Ruhe redden Kann

Mit Leipzigsleute

Nicht heute

Another Day

I am capable
Of atrocity
Capable
When all is said and done
Of rape
Of torturing the innocent
Capable of walking up to a café
Filled with family and friends
And blowing them to
Kingdom come
With
Stoic calm
Capable of celebrating
My own son
For maiming
Children
On the run
Or babies
In the womb
Of laying flowers
On his tomb —
As capable of hate
As love

And if
In that frame of mind
I approach one
Who sees me as
Just another Jew
Just one more
American
One more figure
To dispatch
What do I do then
To enhance
My chance
For inner peace
And harmony

Do I take him out
Serenely

Or allow my anger
To explode
And smite the bastard
Where he stands
And all like him
That ever killed
And raped
And smiled thereafter
As they sipped their tea

And admit
That my pathway to enlightenment
Has hit one more
Impediment

And greet the morrow
Thankful

That I can search for wholeness
Another day

A Garden Toad is Better than a Liebestod

The problem with great passion
Is that it has to end somewhere
And for some it seems
The greater than anticipation
The greater the devastation
When the quotidian intrudes again

Better to lapse out at the very top
Than to drop back to the mondaine
You remember what it's like to soar
And you want more and more
To seek flowers of perfect blue
On some distant shore
To scale jagged mountain peaks
To splinter heaven's doors

When Monet felt the need to paint blue flowers
He planted some in his backyard
Exactly in the place he felt that they should go
Midst others commonplace and rare
And then he got his canvas out
And sketched what had become
The natural scene…
The pictures are by all accounts sublime

After such passion come quietude
The blue of paint that pales the mid-day sun

Whitman found awe in the grass beneath his feet
He didn't need to die to feel complete

Icarus

The fishermen, so the story goes,
Did not see Icarus fall into the waves
They were too busy mending their nets
Or pulling in their catch
That's what the painter tried to convey
When he rendered the scene in epic scale
And sold it to the city for display
In a space where thousands passed every single day
A striking work the critics all agreed
One person glanced
Last year
He did indeed

By Words Alone

In the wilderness
Metaphors
Burst forth from thorn bushes
Like divine fire
That
Once noticed
Seize upon you
Like a calling

And
Stammer though you may
There is no mistake

You are the one chosen
To draw forth nations from the sand
To celebrate the parting of the waves
To sojourn on mountaintops
To turn Thunder into verses
Carved in stone

To slake the thirst of multitudes
By words alone

Rage rises in your throat —
To have been thought
So adequate
And you strike hard
Instead
Your wooden staff
Now turned to lead

The people will wend their way
A lesser poet at their head
As you turn back to face
The desert wind
And lisp your dreams of promise
To the dead

In a Rhetorical Mode

for Yitzhak Rabin, in memoriam

Words are supposed to move mountains
And men
That's one of the things that words are for
And when one such man is moved
And grabs a gun and shoots to kill
We say
No
That is not what we meant at all
When we said kill
It was a metaphor
For vigorous complaint
That's all
Collective action at the polls…
You should have known
You stupid shit
Why don't you go off
And end it all
You
Not me
I meant that
Metaphorically
Of course

Now that you've finally understood
Come help me clean up all this blood

The Limits of Art

…and, as I danced,
even as I danced
(quite well, by the way,
someone who knows that kind of thing
said), an A-
rab with a long knife but-
chered four women in
Jerusalem (if I forget thee,
oh…) shouting, G-
od is great, in
iambic pentameter, e-
ven as the blood splat-
tered to the ground
(to make a point, he
said), even as I danced,
eeeeeee-
ven
as I dance
still.

No Sweat

To Amadee Ardoin, may he rest in peace

So I asked him where he made his big mis-
take and he looked at me straight and he said,
You want to know how I got here, dead?
And then he poured himself a shot of whis-
key, yeah; they got it there, if you must know.
I got here, for true, cause I sweat a lot.
Them white clubs I played in, they gets real hot.
We played real sweet, and it wern't long befo'
That sweat be pourin' down like a warta-
fall. I made no mind, you hear, just played dat fiddle,
Till somewhere on round about the middle
Dis white chick up and wiped my brow, I oughta
Knowed that dat would do it. Dem white boys, dey let
You be, jes' as long as dey don' see you sweat.

Dance Notes

I

It is the same flesh
Now extended
Lifting
Turning full circles
Yesterday
Earthbound
The same flesh
Shoulder to finger tips
Dangling
Purposeless sinews siding
Inert meat

Manoeuvers unfolding in sequence
Controlled enthusiasm, ex-
Hileration, ex-
Uberance

The others go through patterns with
Professional calm
While I tremble
Silently
Thrust skyward
And turn
Madness in courtly dress
Moving to a piper's call

II

The person is unknown to me in
All but the leap skyward
And yet I handle her
Grasp her flesh with im-
Personal intimacy
Place her here,
There

We make our adjustments
As the form demands
And we both know when it
All went well
As after an act of love

We separate
Court others in passing
Return

And we both know when it
All went well
As after an act of love

III

A change of music brings a
Change of style,
Personality, bearing, soul-
Projections, fantasies, trans-
formations in discrete
Packages of sound.

Underneath it all
One discrete individual
Shorn of all
Poses
Somewhere —
Or just
The dance

Daredevil Poetry

This poem is not like a motorcycle
Poised
To charge up a ramp
And soar
Over an abyss
To land
Just at the lip
On the far side
And spin triumphantly
To a stop

This poem
In fact
Could fail
In whole or part
And still the poet would survive
To try the ramp
Another day

A poem is not a struggle for life
Or death
All hanging
On the proper timing
Of a metaphor

And yet
The thrill is there
And the suspense
The call
To soar over an expanse
Is irresistible

I look straight ahead
I feel the purr of the engine's power
Between my legs
And I go for it
Time and time again

It gets into my blood
It does
To cross gullies and gorges
In a single verse
To head for Arizona
At long last
To take the Grand Canyon
With inches to spare
And ride off
The desert wind
Whipping through my hair
And tomorrow
To return
My hands waving wildly in the air
And reach the other side
Perhaps
Or crash and burn

Derelict

His name is Charles Jeeter
And he wanted to be remembered
(Don't we all)
He lived
In the Bowery
In flop houses
In and out of alcoholic haze
Until at fifty
Someone gave him an old tape player
And a mike
And asked him to narrate his life story
And those of others like himself
For
Posterity
And that had a nice ring to it
It did
And he stuck to this one task
The first time in his life
And thanked his God
For letting him be born
For letting him survive
Until that day

I listened to his tape
I cried —
To feel that sense of gratitude
Just once
Before I died

Ducktown, Tennessee

You can't just cover red clay with a mess of trees
At least not the hills that I recall
The hills we climbed to look down on the slag pond
The hills we slid down in winter when the snows came
The hills that told you you were almost home
When you caught your first glimpse of them after a long trip
Anywhere

The hills we showed our children
To tell them how it was
Back then
When we worked the mines

They are reclaiming these hills
They say
To repair an injury to the earth
For our children
And our children's children
They say

And the green creeps closer

Until one day
Our town will be like all the rest
You couldn't pick it out from the air at all
Unless you really know

I reckon when the time comes
They will dig through the grass
And bury me in the red clay
I'll know then
That I'm home

Fanny Mendelssohn - Opus II

The face that stares out at you is the picture
Of Innocence
What the men then assumed
All women
To be like
At the heart
Capable of evanescent feelings
Vague longings
Poesy

Songs perhaps
Not symphonies
Not —
This

The music that poured from her pen
Exudes such confidence
Such workmanship
Such fire
It is no wonder
It lay unplayed
A hundred years and more

I struggle through the notes and ponder
If I found a soul
With such a face
Would I adore her from afar
Write sonnets to her
Immortalize her name
Or walk her through some muck and mire
To see if ought remained
Of innocence and grace

This lass
Who stayed within the rules of dress
Exemplifying
Loveliness
Carved out these notes from adamantine stone

The piece is far beyond my ken
I sweat and strain
I struggle through the score
Again
Again
Until I can play no more
Never will I be
Quite woman enough
To savor
Such heady stuff

Les Feuilles Mortes

Slow autumnal fires
Warm me
At every turn
Even as the air chills

The leaves will waft
All too soon
Upon the wind
Crisp
And crumble

My knees grumble
As I dance
Steps learned
Many years ago

I burn
I glow
I grey
Embering with November joy

I am rushing to a fall
Naked branchedly —
Barest memories of green —
Deciduously savoring
All that I have ever seen

Cherry Blossoms in October

Perhaps it was just confused
This one cherry tree
And thought it might be spring
Perhaps it wondered why
There were no bees
There it stood
In full blossom
Midst others
Whose leaves were turning red

I am in the autumn of my life
They say
Preparing for winter's cold
The days are getting shorter
I look skyward
I let a few buds open to the sun
One aging tree
Out of season
Beyond rime and reason
Waiting to bear fruit
In late December

Final Descent

There are three ways of getting down
Over the last ridge
At Lion's Head

One slopes gently
Meanders
Asks little of you
As you wend your way
Slowly
Down

One asks of you
Only
What you think
You know

And one asks more

That you push yourself
Over the edge
With the very end in sight
Over new terrain

Icy
Slick
And
Steep
Somehow
You will get down
(You cannot stay)
And make a mental note
That you could have done far more
Before
To prepare
To make of this last ordeal
Something
Far more casual
And sweet

Like
Gliding gracefully
Toward death
Instead of yielding
Inch by inch
Twisted and tight
Maladroit

As if you have never danced before
Or felt the wind
Caress
Your face

For the Sheer Joy

No bees
But still they blossom
In November cold
White azaleas
Narcissi
And a single marigold

We
Fruit no more
But still we blossom
In cold November
In January
The beginning of another year
For the sheer joy of flowering
For the sheer joy
Of
Opening
To the winter sun

For the Residents of Greenbriar at the Altamount

Just Me

If you tell me
When you see the pain in my face
That the children that died last year from AIDS
Were part of a Divine plan
That we will come to understand
In the end of days —

If you tell me it was their Karma
To suffer just that way —

I will tell you
Not to come to my house
For tea
I would rather drink alone again
Just me

Nameless

An old Greek lady tells me
I dance like her grandfather
From an island
I have never seen
I look at her and say
Efaristo
She smiles back and says
Parikalo
And the music plays on
I have heard it before
I know it like I know my own name
(Which someone once told me
Is a Celtic word for spear)
When I dance
I have no name
I am from an island
I have never seen
Perhaps back then
I was a fisherman

The Poet

If you try to get the feeling right
The poem
Ails
To that extent
The meter and the metaphor
Languish
If they have to serve the truth
He wrote
Struggling to be precise —
Exquisite verse
I marveled as he read aloud
Thin voiced, yet strangely
Sonorous
Did I detect a note of sorrow moving through a
Tone of wistfulness —
The shabby coat he always wore
The thinning hair
A tremor
Barely visible
In his slightly twisted hand
And the uneven gait —
No, I'll let the poem be
I'll let you speculate
The poet reads
As he is wont to do
In a small café
On a near-deserted street
Off
In a corner of my mind
Indeed
I do prevaricate
It's just that
His style
Is just
So hard
To emulate

Poetry Does Not Come Cheap

Poetry does not come cheap
Last week
It took the death of four
To rouse my muse
To start the stream of words aflowing
The structure of ideas growing
To interpose the passions, to infuse
Meaning at the core
To transform a shriek
Into something beauteous and deep.

No, poetry does not come cheap
It takes spilled blood, at times, to make me peek
Over the edge, into the abyss, gore
To let me lose
Myself, the images glowing
In the dark night of my soul, slowing
To a stately dance whose
Steps finally are more
Composed than bleak —
I'd rather sing than weep,

But poetry does not come cheap.
Broken bodies reek
On the shower house floor
I stand, I shout and I accuse
My mind is tearing; my tongue is going,
Slow, the measured lyrics of my poem showing
Through in somber hues —
Until, at last, the words begin to soar
To light the sky, a meteor streak.
But poetry does not come cheap

Predator and Prey

When all is said and done
Predators get fed
They wait by water holes and springs
They pick off the weak, the wounded
The unaware
While we
Amble on our way
As if amiability were an amulet
To ward off
Catastrophe
As if cheerfulness masked the fact
That we are
Meat —
Poet
Statesman
Engineer —
Meat
Penetrable by glass and claw
Easily combustible

Predators sleep long hours every day
They conserve their energy
They loll in shadows
Until their hunger
Wakes

Poets
Statesmen
Engineers —
Stalked in turn by
Leopards
Jackals
By madmen and specialists
Who savor death
Like wine
To sip
Or swill
They surround us

Calculate the right angle of approach
Draw blood
Kill
They eat their fill
Till there is nothing left of us at all
But the memory of the sounds we make
As we fall —
Poets
Statesmen
Engineers
Babies in the womb
Couples walking in the woods

Food

To Isaac Stern

In memoriam

It was
An answer
To terror
The sweet sounds
Of a 250 year old
Violin
In a concert hall
In Israel
Played for an audience
Wearing gas masks
By a master
Wearing a gas mask
As children painted flowers
On gas masks
And slept
And got up
And went to school
And played some more.

Reprinted from *Jewish Reel*

Wiedergutmachenangelegenheit

In the darkest cave
The blind retain
An image of the sun
Pale creatures hatched at midnight
Grope
Searching for a pun

Complex molecules are born
To teach the world to dance
Complex words luxuriate
Beyond all happenstance

A verb bursts forth at sunrise
A noun explodes at noon
A recompense for anguish
Before the day is done

While the Old Men Dance

*for Wellington Arnaud, Tom Bozighian, Running Bear, Beverly Bishop, and
all those who know what it is to watch old men (and old women) dance.*

Minds
Yielding to the body's wisdom,
They tread ancient paths
To an ancient beat —
Slowly circling the spot
Where the earth and heavens meet
      The young bucks
      In their separate space
      Work up a sweat
      Stomping on the crust of earth
      As if dust were concrete

While the old men dance
While the old men
Dance

Olé

to Teresa and her troop

They played this music in the dark of night
Fugitives
All
In caves
In a sacred mountain
In memory of exiled folk
The castanets echoing the clash of swords
Dark harmonies
Like the screams of martyrs burning at the stake
Like the moans of women bringing life forth into
Such a world
There
At the edge of endless pits
Where corpses lie in rows
In the middle of the killing fields
Two steps from the crematoria
The full face of horror
Telling to stop
Telling you to turn away

You might not guess that from the steps themselves
They are difficult enough to learn
And to get the body
Just so
There is effort enough involved
Without the history

But there you are anyway
And eventually the music insinuates itself into your brain
It works its way into the soul
Into the very molecules of being

And before long
You stand there
Shorn of everything you thought you were
And could never be
The slope of your back traces

The lines of ancient trees
The movements of your hips
Your breasts
Your thighs
Draw sighs
From children killed before their time
The clap of your hands echoes the heartbeat of the earth
The sun draws light from the fire in your eyes
And distant galaxies swirl
To celebrate
The circle of your arms

Missing Moguls

I prepared myself for bumps and ruts
For all the hill's proclivities
And then awoke to find
That they had smoothed the slope for
Such as me
Whose fantasies oft-times
Outrace agility

Routine descent
Into uncertainty
I prepare myself
For another hill
Another morning
Across the unsmoothed slopes
Of my own proclivities

Mariposa

The poison I consumed
Keeps me safe
It lets me flash my brilliance to the world
I flit here and there
According to a plan
I cannot intimate

I am in transit
I am headed for a place that I have never seen
My children will get closer
Their children may get there
And start the cycle once again

There is sweetness here
Brief passion
Long
Death

I consumed enough poison in my youth
To last a lifetime
It keeps me safe
It lets me flash my brilliance to the world

There is a plan
I cannot intimate

I am in transit
I will die en route
But there is sweetness here
Enough sweetness
To last
A lifetime

Old Trees

Old trees are gnarled
Burled
Bored into
Scarred by lightning
And messages of former lovers
One look will tell you they have character

My bark is mottled now
My limbs creak
My trunk won't flex
It's getting so
The image of myself I see reflected
In the stream below
Is strangely alien

But when the breezes blow
I dance the dance that I have come to know
However slow

Others shake their heads
And talk of where I've been
They talk of aging
Incipient decay
I say nothing in reply
The dance is where I am
Today
Gnarled
Burled
Scarred by lightning
As it were

Developing
Character

The Poet Jeremiah

Anguish, Jeremiah felt, agony
Bursting from his throat, battering his brain
Cries from the Temple Mount, completely insane,
Demented, deafening cacophony
Etched eternally in his every thought.
Festering images, fragmented faces,
Gashed, gory bodies of children, places
Most holy, wholly razed. A horror wrought
Indelibly in a sin-filled nation's heart —
Jeremiah groaned judiciously and
Killed a scream rising in his throat. He planned
The Lamentations line by line and part by part —
Metrical, alphabetical, terse and tight.
No poet rants and raves when he can write.

Perspective

For mosquitoes at dawn
A poet is just
Another source of blood

Second Fall in Birmingham, Alabama

Leaves burn brightly
And are not consumed
There is a message here
Almost a prophecy
Celebrate the color of slow demise
The sheer exuberance of dying

The days grow shorter
Moments of daylight
Shrink into glimpses of emptiness

The voice gets louder

Be autumnal
Burn brightly as the air grows crisp and cold
Let others share
The color of your falling
Your calm exuberance

Dance upon the wind
A winter song on your lips
That a child might sing
Wading through piles of crunchiness

Swirled to the ground
In momentary ecstasy
Beyond all thought of Spring

To Helen

Have you seen yourself dance,
O Helen of the North Country
(Graceful as a willow wand
Bending in the breeze)

Have you cut across the crests
Of whistling white halls
(Lovely as a falling leaf)
Felt the rush of crisp dry air
Deep within your chest
Brushed past trees
(Brittle-cold)
Cut figures in the snow

Have you raced headlong down a mountain ridge
Smiling at the man below
Whose weight you've borne
These many years
Smiling at the solid flesh you've spawned
Smiling quietly within
As the snow melted in your hair

The song of winter birds
Plays across your lips
As you warm the space before you
Minister to all in turn
And turn to face the darkness
Quietly within

Small slip of a girl still
Tender as a willow wand
Waiting for the Spring.

Surprise

Who knows how long he lurked there in the shadows
Before he dashed out among us
Moving from one haven to another
Leaving us speechless for a while

We thought ourselves safe
Protected
High above the street with all its crime
High above the gutters clogged with
The detritus the mud the slime
The collected effluvia of a city that care forgot
Moving toward the sea

We were moved by the muse
To celebrate the power of words
Moved at time to the edge of sheer delight
Only to be reminded once again
That even in the midst of the eternal struggle
To find food, to bring forth a new generation
There are those who wouldn't hesitate a moment
To do us in
To drop our bodies unceremoniously
Into the nearest receptacle

I guess even a rat at times had need of poetry

A Tale of Two Cities

You could live several lifetimes
In sections of Calcutta
And never see an outstretched hand
A drawn face, a belly distended
Extended over spindly legs

Lyric poems blossom in the spring
And cascade in summer like bougainvillea over walls
They lie in autumn like honeyed fruit on silver trays
Like odes in Capetown looking o'er the sea
Like sonnets ambling through manicured gardens
On hills around the city of angels

While ballads sprout
Midst fah-fee runners
In shabeens
Rolling over the tongues of
Tsosties in Sophia town
In Harlem
On the pier
In the city of angels
On Saturday night
Sometimes with a Spanish flair
Sometimes Oriental
Amerindian
Black
The words sizzle
Crack

Poets with an urban beat
Poets that will never meet

Tamburitzan

They played the music
Macedonian
Serbian
Croatian
As if there had been no
Crusaders
No civil strife
No ethnic cleansing
No gang rape
No genocide

And people dance
Makedonskii
Srbskii
Hrvatskii

They danced their way through history
As if their joy could transcend
The memory of loss and pain

As if we could all touch each other
Once again

They danced gypsy
Turkish
Greek

My spirit soared
At least half a week

To Fran

You are
The very center of my life
The touchstone about which
My universe revolves

It has been so
Since the day
You agreed
To share a path with me
Through swamps and
Mountain passes

Same say our union was
Beshert*

Perhaps mere recognition of
Possibility
A spark of wisdom
In early morning light

Perhaps an act of grace
In the vast expanse of space

Does one thank the sun
For coloring clouds at dusk
Or just watch
Amazed
As pink turns gray

Celebrate the moment
With child delight
Then meander
Hand in hand
Toward
Night

*predistined

To Live Fully

To live fully one must keep the vines trimmed
The ones that proliferate along subterranean roots
And shoot up twenty feet into the air
Until they find our branches and cling and foliate
Blanketing everything with their own green celebration
Until there is only a memory of our own flowering

Weeds herald spring weeks before the grass
Given half a chance
Like water hyacinths in a pond
Like kudzu in a field
Like cancer crowding into hidden places

To live fully one must keep the vines trimmed
The strangling fig that girds about the middle
And then clothes us so completely
There's not an inch of skin left
Exposed to remind us of Eden

Our fields are filled with thorns and thistles
Weeds grow robustly
We mow
We edge and shape and cut and slash and pull
We edit so completely
Contain the energy so discretely

To live fully
One must keep the vines trimmed

Two Icons—Reflections on Tinos, 35 Years Later

They pass it without a second glance
That icon there
A museum piece for sure
It has no business being here
Where pilgrims pass to catch a glimpse
To kiss the other one
The one that tears
The one that cures
Thankfully
Covered by gold and jewels
To hide the lack of artistry

The pious do not ponder or assess
They drop a crutch or two
They start to procreate
To see again
The one that tears

The other one is dulled by dirt and dust
Its maker by his very genius
Cursed

Variations on a Theme by Gretel Gunsing

for Teresa Romero Torkanowsky
for Irene

Remember
Before the first note sounds
Before the ritual unfolds again
You are not just any person
Struggling to open..
You are Eve
Crying out with sheer delight
At the first dusk
At the first dawning
Celebrating hips
And thighs
And toes
Celebrating
Fingertips
You draw the very heavens into your womb
And in pain and laughter
You give birth to life itself
You are every woman that has ever loved
Every woman that has bared her bosom to the rain
Every woman that has ached as the cord is cut
That has held her child up to the sun
And sung lullabies to the growing darkness
Every woman that has shared her sisterhood with the moon
And measured the flow of her own blood against the tides
You are not just any person
Struggling to open to the Spring
You are Eve dancing in the garden
Flowers open to greet you as you pass
Trees thrust upward to the clouds
Your arms retrace the whirl of galaxies
At the dawn and dusk of time
And your eyes flash fire

The Philosophy of Purple

for Zom

Philosophy is born of early pain.
Children huddled in dark corners, alone.
Trying to make sense of a world insane;
Battered and abused, trying to atone
For what was done to them in fits of rage,
Trying to correct the world they know,
To flee somehow the anguish of the cage
To bleed inside and say it isn't so.

Children romping over the crest of a knoll
Don't need to question why bodies roll down-
Hill, why leaves show brilliantly before they
Fall, why birds sing sweetly as the winds of winter
Call. They drink deeply till the water is all gone,
And paint purple on what they're told is grey.

Manifesto II

They thought the odor was wafted from somewhere
Over the fence
But it was right there under the back leg of the chair
In the middle of the patio
A fresh turd of canine origin
Insinuating itself between the verses
Phrases
Words
So that at the very moment the poet spoke
Of the blossoming of her great aunt's madness
From the excrement of the dogstar
In the center of the universe
We got a whiff
Of that self-some stuff

And is this not what generations of poets have said

Words that can only flow in perfumed patios
Like the songs of bejeweled birds
May titillate the senses of Chinese emperors
On their morning jaunts
But we folk require something somewhat funky
Colors that assault the eye
And invade the nostrils
Like doggy doo
Like the rotting corpses of old whores and young warriors
Underfoot, sticking to the shoe, tracking on the rug
Lingering memories of powerful moments
Of poetry
Joyously
Olfactory

Zapatec

The earth
If one searches well
Contains a range of pastel hues
Enough to translate all the old designs
Onto new walls
Half a world away
      Savage bards
      Trained to sing
      Spontaneously
      In ballad form
      For city folk
      To catch a glimpse of
      How it was assumed to be
      At the very dawn of history
The dyes are all natural,
The salesman says
One would almost expect to see
Mauves and taupes
Insinuate into the hills of Mexico
      Snow
      Tutored by Impressionists
      To lie
      In purple drifts
      Under blue-orange trees
Pesos growing like
Cactus in Zapatec
Indians dancing joyfully
Swirling serapes of
Beige and lavender

Greek Fest

New Orleans, 2013

Under the sun's glare
Alpha and Omega play a Tsamikos
And I open up
Like Buddha
On a lotus flower

How many steps to climb Olympus
To stand at Sinai
And then to dance
Cavort around the altar
Come what may

David leapt and twirled
Past Uza's tomb
And Micah's frown
And for one moment
Suspended in the air
A bottle poised neatly on his head
He found
Peace

Gratitude

The snake was blessed
She led us to our
Humanity

There was no fear of death in
Eden
No
Mortality
Exclamations of delight
Perhaps
But certainly
No
Poetry

I do not long for lost
Innocence
I am aware of my own
Nakedness
Aware of time and
Shame

Were it not for death
These lines would have remained
Follicular

I revel in life of Wednesdays
Midway
Between the Shabbatot
Womb and
Tomb

I plant seeds that often
Molder
Write poems that often
Flounder
Approaches to my wife
Founder

Sometimes I dance quietly
Around her

The serpent foresaw
She fulfilled her purpose
Now she slithers

I celebrate my yearning
The emptiness that frames my passion
I cloak myself in tears and
Laughter
I have no need to think of a
Hereafter

On Our Own

Ultimately
We are put upon
This earth
To screw
Everything
Else we do
Is on our own

The Whisper and the Roar

for Chris Champagne
and Mel Brooks ...and Rabelais

There is a beauty that rests softly on the tongue
Like the memory of fine champagne
That whispers like asters in evening
Like Zen gardens in purple haze

There is a beauty that surges like a mountain stream
That fills the mouth to overflowing
That drips down the chin
Like the syrup of roasted yams
That dances wildly at the edge of deep ravines
That snatches laughter from bellies
That shouts raucously from steeple tops...
Here I am
Ready or not
And there are you as well

I sit quietly in my rock garden
The mists of morning coalesce
Dangling delicately from a single strand of spider silk
And I recall the surge
The gasp
The fall
The utter, utter splendor of it all

While a fat toad zaps a tse tse fly on Lao Tze's toe
And Buddha roars

Life and Art

It takes me days to write a poem
He said
And when at last I'm done I realize
That I've lived through more than I could write in ten
The more I do the further back I get
It is a paradox, he said
And I agreed
Perhaps it would do well to stop
Living at this place a while, he said
Just to catch up
I'll stay in my room
Walled up
Like a monk in his cell
Contemplative
I'll have my meals brought in
Unplug the phone, the radio, TV
Close the shutters
Be celibate, for a while at least
Just until my words catch up with what I've seen
And where I've been

Interesting, I said
Worth at least a verse or two
Or more
The process
The experience
Your vision shaped day by day
Honed by the hour
Undamped by the hurly burly of the outside world

He scowled once and then he snarled
You did that to me again
I nodded absentmindedly
Breakfast at Mad Dog's I asked

It's always lively there, he said
Something worth writing about
Perchance

Next year
I'm booked till then, he said
And scowled anew

The trouble with you, I said
Is that you enjoy life too well
He nodded, then he snarled again
And on the way for coffee and croissants
Three long poems were conceived —
I couldn't tell if he was angry or relieved

Art and Politics

They played Verdi in Theresienstadt —
For a while — gaunt and bony-fingered —
The sounds arose — the musicians lingered —
Pampered just a bit — a month or so — then shot,
Or gassed and burned — it really mattered not
Once they were selected out. Tones even
That might 'ope the rusted doors of heaven
Could not derail for long a führer's plot.
Beauty may set military feet tapping.
It may caress the palate like aged wine —
While connoisseurs re-create a state — judenrein —
Listen to fists on shower doors — rapping —
And hand the violins on down the line,
Trusting the next concert will be just fine.

Sprecher

My grandfather was a Sprecher
He was prone
For a modest fee
To free a home of demons
On nights
When the west wind blew
He could hypnotize
With a phrase or two
Pressing a knife
Flat against the brow —
To lift the spirits —
To restore the soul

I am often
At a loss for words
On windy nights
In this very poem
I search in vain
With feverish brow
For a phrase or two
To ease the pain —
Without a knife
To call my own

Yawping with Whitman

I saw Walt Whitman in Orlando
It was on the Fourth of July
Old greybeard walking amidst the crowds
Gathered to see fireworks light up the sky
His barbaric yawp blended in with the
        cheers and shouts
As the chrysanthemums blossomed briefly
As the bombs burst in air

This is America he said
Tattooed and pierced, tawny and pale, dark
        as midnight
Sari-ed and sarong-ed, braided and
        dredlocked
Turbaned, kerchiefed
Dancing boogaloo, salsa, calypso
Tuned in to gangsta rap
And Händel and Koto and Gaida
They're all here gawking at those bits of
        metallic oxides
Purple, green, pink and white

One sings God Bless America
Another This Land is Your Land
Berlin and Woody meeting down by the
        riverside
And Walt just clapping away

It's already the 17th of Tammuz
Thoughts of death and destruction
Guilt
Atonement
Filtering through my brain

And Walt slaps me on the back and says
Isn't it all grand
And I'm knee-deep in children racing around
Oohing and aahing, scared by the noise

Sleeping on their father's arms
Puking up popcorn
Snarfing up hotdogs and cotton candy
And hasn't it been almost a year
Since the twin towers fell
People letting themselves feel safe enough
To celebrate being here and now
And wow, Walt is taking off his shoes and socks
Feeling the leaves of grass and mud between his toes

Dancing a dance so old it doesn't have a name
Something Eve did in the garden
After Adam plucked her rose or ate the fruit
And became fully man

The chemistry is here

Chinese, Italian, American
Spread out across the sky

Somewhere else

Placed in a truck
Near a market or a school
Set to blow sky high
To splatter red

Here red gives way to green
And blue
And Walt is everywhere
Running his fingers through people's hair
Splashing them with amorous wet
Yawping
Till the crowd is gone
Another birthday
America
He smiles and waves
Hasta la vista
Salaam
Shalom

Just Before Waking

for Don Hong Oai

The poem sits on the palm
Like a toad that
Once released
Hops
Plumply
Under a tangle of thorns
Just before waking

In Which the Poet Views His Present
and Future As a Jellyfish

carried
currently
assimilating bits of life that
happen by
shedding seed
here and there
almost transparent
waived at last
sand dead
on a distant shore
almost opaque
almost ready
to be picked at
clawed
assimilated
bit by bit
by
any life that
happens by
at piece

My Unlawn

A lawn is
Uniformly green
At least that is the intent
My neighbors think as much
And pay
To have all species but one
Suppressed
Eradicated
Undone

Their lawns
Pristine
While mine —

For all I know
Seeds from Madagascar and Japan
Take refuge
Here
Weeds from every corner of the globe

Honeysuckles grow wildly over bushes
Smother them with
Fragrance

A bit of Pollock
In a world gone
Mondrian

The minute blooms that
Proliferate

Purple, white and gold
Whose names I do not know
That crowd out the grass
Soothe my soul
In the trees above
Birds sing choruses of
Pleasing cacophony

I celebrate
Randomness
Diversity
To balance out
Monochromobidinous
Propensities

Pyla, Cyprus

The only place on the whole island
An island on the island
Where people prevailed over
Power
And politics
What others might call
Common sense

That Turks and Greeks
Could live together
In apparent
Harmony

Some might call it
Treachery

Like Jews and Moslems
In Neve Shalom
A dot
An island
In a troubled sea

On searches for such islands around the globe
Perhaps a village in Karachi
A neighborhood in Belfast
A township near Johannesburg
There must be places
Where sworn enemies
Are just neighbors
Albeit
With different faiths
And different mother tongues

I speak about this matter
With a Russian Jew
Who lives there
In Pyla

He assures me
It is true
The town is in a buffer zone
A no-man's land
Close to a Greek city
Ceded to the Turks
And now deserted

And I think
That our tour of Cyprus has been
Misguided

We have seen the wonders
That tourists seek out
The museums
The beaches
The mountain peaks
The ornate churches
The mosque —
Where legend has it
That Mohammed's wet nurse
Fell off her mule
And died —
The flamingos on the salt lake

The barriers in Nicosia
Barrels filled with sand
Barbed wire
Separating
Children

But I missed seeing
Pyla
Perhaps the greatest wonder of them all

It got scant mention
In our guidebook
A few lines
Among so many pages

And it is Pyla
Whose name should echo
Through the years
One of the seven wonders
Of the world

I mused in passage
A small dot on the map
Off the beaten track
I will know better
I say
If I ever return
This way
If I ever

I have said that before
My life marked
More
By what I have missed
Than by what I have seen

In passage
Always in passage
Looking for an island
Where I can find
Peace

The Heart of the Matter — the Gall

Like an old car
The parts wear out
One by one
The iron lady
Rusts
And I as well
I see it in my skin
Blotched and
Mottled
An outward sign
Of what breaks down
Within

My mother put it well
At ninety
Her mind unimpaired
Alert
Aware
Her body
A near total catastrophe
How did I get here
She said
I still feel young

Life
Terminates
The center will not hold
We stand
At the edge of the abyss
And wonder
What it has all meant
Beyond the journey itself
Beyond the people
Who have walked beside us
Whose hands we have held
Whose words we have heard
Whom we have birthed
And nurtured —

The music we have played
The dances we have danced

We wheeze our way
Toward some black hole
Some junkyard
Where our parts
Perhaps
Will be salvaged
To keep another motor running

While pious souls
Nibble at platitudes and
Sate themselves with the promise
Of the dawn
Of yet
Another day

In My Own Time

I will not race
Against another
I will not compete

However long it takes
I will do things
In my own time

Which shrinks
Day by day
I can see that
In my face

I cram works
Colors
Notes
Into a box
Of unknown size
And hope the sides won't burst
Strewing everything
For the wind to take
Morsels for ants to feast upon
Assimilate
Digest
Leaving little piles of excrement
To fertilize
Purple thistles
Ragweed
Or perhaps
A rose

Faint fragrance
In a distant place

***

www.ingramcontent.com/pod-product-compliance
Lightning Source LLC
Chambersburg PA
CBHW060314260626
47160CB00007B/2603